# DEAR HUNTER,

# DEAR HUNTER,

Letters from Father to Son

MATTHEW DIGERONIMO

FIRST EDITION

ISBN: 979-8-71-075184-8

Library of Congress Control Number: 2021904980

www.mattdigeronimo.com

*This book is dedicated to my dear son, Hunter.*

# *A*cknowledgements

Thank you to the following people for making this book possible:

Caroline Heskett for your unwavering love and support

Theresa DiGeronimo for your editorial assistance
and for authoring the foreword of this book

Colleen DiGeronimo for your book cover design

Emily Lipski for your editorial assistance

# *F*oreword

The foreword of any book is generally skipped right over by the reader, eager to get to the actual book—the main meal. Yet, a book's foreword has an important job to do. It's like the pre-dinner conversation that sets up the tone and direction of the time that will be spent together and gives the larger context in which to better understand and appreciate what you're about to engage in.

In this case, the larger context that gives background and insight to the meat of this book is my understanding of the author—my son. Where does this advice that he offers his son come from? How has he developed his world view? What are the chances that the lessons he desires to pass on to his son are sound and helpful?

The truth is that reading these letters has left me dumbstruck, asking myself these very questions. Of course, all parents offer years of lessons and advice in the hope of giving their children the skills and knowhow they need to be safe, happy, and at peace. I, myself, offered my son advice about life, success, failure, happiness, sorrow, relationships, and so on and on. Then, as the day of leaving home to begin his independent adult life at college grew closer and closer, I worried about practical things: Does he know how to do laundry? Can he sew on a fallen button? Will he be responsible with a credit card? Does he know how to navigate mass transit? Oh, the worries were endless and rooted in my gut realization that there was so much more for him to learn—I had not covered it all.

Now, these many years later, as I read through these letters, written with such raw honesty and humility, I find that, as I suspected, it was not I who taught him the most important life lessons—life itself did that. I've learned so much about his previously unspoken hurts, challenges, obstacles, and disappoints, as well as triumphs and accomplishments, that have kneaded him into the man he is today—a good, kind, and loving spouse, father, son, and friend. It seems that through his own relentless efforts he has found himself, as I had always hoped: safe, happy, and at peace. Standing on this strong foundation, he now has the wisdom and perspective needed to give fatherly advice that is philosophical and practical, tender and harsh, funny and brutal, contrite and proud.

No doubt, life has many lessons waiting to share with you, dear Hunter, that no one can give you in advance—not even your dad. But having this book at your side gives you a superpower in your life's journey. You have physical, hold-in-your-hand proof of the immeasurable depth of his love. When alone, when in doubt, when unsure, go to this book. Yes, it has good advice and offers excellent guidance that will serve you well in many life situations, but, most importantly, it is concrete evidence that you are loved, you are important. This book is your warm, safety blanket as you seek out new adventures. Keep it always nearby and, as your dad tells you at the very end of this book, you will never tremble in the cold.

*Theresa DiGeronimo*
"Grandma"

# $\mathcal{P}$reface

*Dear Hunter*

I hope this letter finds you with a peaceful mind. As I write this first letter in a series of letters contained in this book, you are not yet three years old and I am forty-seven. The past three years have changed my life's perspective more than I ever could have imagined. From witnessing the miracle of birth, to watching you grow, learn, and develop at a breakneck speed, to basking in the daily joy that just being in your presence has provided - I've experienced a rebirth of my own. That rebirth was accompanied by a seamless shifting of life priorities. I've always been the main character in the movie of my life, but now I know that my true role is a supporting character in the movie of your life, and I am overjoyed at the opportunity.

I've spent many nights lying awake in bed thinking about how to best support you. I've heard it said that your children will forget what you tell them but will always remember what you did. Actions speak louder than words - I get that. But I also know that I have so much to tell you. I want to share with you, in an impactful way, the life lessons that I had to learn the hard way. In this book, you will find letters that contain my best effort to share with you some life lessons that I have learned. It is my hope and deepest wish that they will serve you well. I suspect that these letters will have varying effects on you at different stages of your life. They say that no man can ever stand in the same river twice. On the second attempt, he will be a different man and the river will be a different river. Each time you read these letters, a new person will be reading them and the words will tell you a new story based on your current life circumstances. The one constant will be my love for you.

I am always on your side, in your corner, and in your heart - always.

*Love,*
*Dad*

# *C*ontents

*Dear Hunter*

Most of the letters contained in this book are, in some form or fashion, my attempts to give you advice. I am under no delusions about the reality of giving life advice to someone—even, or especially, to my own son. For better or worse, most advice falls on deaf ears. Still, this letter is about advice—how to receive it, how to give it, and how to think about it.

Sound advice is typically grounded in life experience. It has been said that good judgment comes from experience and experience comes from bad judgment. I'm not sure I agree with that expression fully, but it makes for a nice saying, and there's a grain of truth embedded within it. Those with more experience typically give the best advice, but what does it really mean "to give good advice"?

One of the soundest pieces of advice I ever received was from my parents when I was 20 years old. I was attending Rutgers University on a full academic scholarship when I got the idea that I should quit school and enlist in the United States Navy. Why? To this day, I'm not sure, but it had something to do with the fact that I had grown bored with college and, candidly, my life. My parents told me pointedly that I would be much better off graduating from college and then pursuing a commission as a Naval Officer if I was hell-bent on joining the Navy. They clearly and respectfully laid out the reasons for their objections. Now and then, their reasoning was bulletproof. They knew me better than I knew myself and wanted nothing but the best for me. I left for Navy boot camp several weeks later— categorically ignoring the advice of my parents.

Why didn't I take my parents' advice? It was solid advice from the people that I trusted and respected more than anyone else on the planet. The perceived stakes to my future, which I did care about deeply, were high, and I was venturing into uncharted territory.

Maybe I ignored the advice because I thought I had all of the answers. I wanted something uncommon, extraordinary, and exciting that the typical college graduate knows nothing of, and I wanted it now. Fast forward 20 years and my decision to enlist in the Navy turned out to be a good and rewarding one. There were certainly moments, especially early on in my service, where I was brought to tears with regret. However, as is often the case, fortune favors the bold. I enjoyed a career in the United States Navy that included finishing my degree in Nuclear Engineering and earning a commission as a Naval Officer. The experiences and life lessons that I gained proved priceless and the memories of the challenges, the missions, and amazing people are among my fondest.

With the benefit of hindsight, was my parents' advice flawed? Did I get lucky? Does fortune actually favor the bold? If so, why do people tend to become less bold with age? The answers boil down to identifying, evaluating, and understanding risk.

Often, risk is viewed as the possibility of something bad happening. However, this is not a particularly useful way to view risk. For example, jumping off the top of a 50-story building is not risky. It is dangerous. The outcome is known. A more accurate way of viewing risk is that it is a measure of the likely variability of the outcome. Most advice, especially the advice of parents whose primal instinct is to protect their offspring, is founded in the desire to avoid negative outcomes more than it is to create positive outcomes. People react more negatively to a loss or a negative outcome than they react positively to an equally sized gain or positive outcome. More plainly, it hurts more to lose 10 dollars than it feels good to win 10 dollars. As we accumulate life lessons and experience the agony of defeat, the likelihood of accepting risk reduces because the retained pain of our losses outweighs the retained pleasure of our victories. This response is the result of our ancestors' desire to stay alive; their definition of a bad outcome was serious injury or death. Avoiding negative outcomes seems like a sound life strategy. However, as the saying goes, "without risk there is no reward." When we decide to reduce the variability of outcomes, or reduce risk, we are also reducing the opportunity for grand victories. Therefore, yes—fortune does favor the bold because only the bold make decisions that allow for enough variability to include fortune as a possible outcome.

In light of this discussion of risk, we can bring the conversation back to advice. When receiving advice from someone, it is imperative that you evaluate the inherent risk aversion that the giver is likely to have. A father is clearly apt to protect his child from harm and, therefore, his advice is likely to contain a high degree of risk aversion. That is not to suggest that my advice will always be overly risk averse, but it is more likely to be than your buddy who lives across town. Keep this in mind. When giving advice, make a point to discuss the risk perspective from which you are coming. What outcomes, both positive and negative, would your advice prevent? What outcomes would they allow?

It is said that opportunity knocks softly. I agree. I would contend that the best advice knocks even more softly. Advice is really any information that you receive from a source that helps you make a decision. Every book you read, every song you hear, every movie that you watch, and every conversation that you have—every bit of information that comes from the outside world into your brain—could potentially be the best piece of advice you will ever receive. Remain open to this possibility. Our minds may be masters at filtering out useless information, but they are imperfect in their task. Train your brain to listen intently to what you are hearing, regardless of the perceived credibility of the source. Life has a funny way of hiding pearls of wisdom in the most unsuspecting places.

Ultimately, the decisions you make are your own. You will make decisions in life that result in negative outcomes—even when you have the opportunity to follow someone's advice to prevent you from doing so. That is okay. In fact, it is inevitable. A bad outcome is not the definition of a bad decision. Decisions that are blind to risk are bad decisions. If you identify the risk in a decision that you are about to make and you can live with the negative outcomes that are possible but are willing to take a chance to capture the grand victory, then you are making a wise decision—even if the outcome isn't the one for which you were hoping.

Some final thoughts on giving and receiving advice:

- Unsolicited advice is rarely, if ever, appreciated. A smart person knows what to say, a wise person knows whether to say it or not. Learn to keep your mouth shut.

- No one likes a "know-it-all." Many people give advice as a way to display their bountiful wisdom. Avoid these people and, please, do not become one.

- World-class advice-giving is done by allowing the person you are speaking with to develop a solution on their own. An insightful question or two will often suffice—the Socratic Method, if you will.

- When your advice is acted upon and the outcome is bad, people remember that it was your advice that was bad. If the outcome is good, they will forget and credit themselves. Buck the trend on this subject. If you followed advice that led to a good outcome remember to give credit and thanks. If you followed advice that led to a bad outcome you own the decision and never imply the contrary.

- Giving advice is not about delivering the "right" answer. In life, there are usually no right or wrong answers. Focus more on your delivery and less on the content. As Maya Angelou once said, "People will forget what you said, but people will never forget how you made them feel."

- Resist the temptation to utter the words, "I told you so"—in any context.

- Always be thankful for advice given to you—whether it was solicited or not. You never know when you will need to rely on this person for their honest opinion in the future, and, if you shut them out, you may not receive it when you need it most.

- Never be too proud to ask for advice. However, don't ask the question if you aren't willing to hear the answer.

*Love,*
*Dad*

*Dear Hunter*

The thought of writing this book scares me—truly. There are not many challenges in life that I find more imposing than the blank page of a computer screen and a blinking cursor. This is not a new feeling to me. Often, when I am faced with a daunting project or goal, I become paralyzed with feelings of inadequacy, self-doubt, and fear that, if left unchecked, will result in inaction and ultimately in no progress. I have no doubt that you will find yourself in similar situations with similar thoughts throughout your life. This is a very common phenomenon. In fact, I would venture to say that most people experience this feeling in some form. Unless we take the time to examine this phenomenon and create strategies for overcoming these feelings, it is likely that our lives will be only a shadow of our true potential.

Les Brown once said, "The graveyard is the richest place on earth because it is here that you will find all the hopes and dreams that were never fulfilled, the books that were never written, the songs that were never sung, the inventions that were never shared, the cures that were never discovered, all because someone was too afraid to take that first step, keep with the problem, or determined to carry out their dream."

Read that quote again, please.

The truth of this quote saddens and shakes me to my core. Life is miraculous and precious, and so are the ideas that our minds spawn. To think of the magnitude of ideas, hopes, and dreams that go unfulfilled—not because of a lack of talent, ambition, or opportunity, but because of fear—is a tragedy. Fear of what? Fear of failure? Fear of rejection? Fear of looking foolish? There are no tigers waiting in the brush to maul us because our ideas, goals, and ambitions aren't good enough. If it wasn't so tragic, it would be hysterical. Make no mistake—we are not talking about weak people. We are talking about people that by all outward appearances are strong, capable, and determined. However, deep inside us is a demon who taunts us with incessant, negative messages of self-doubt aimed at convincing us to keep our heads down and follow the crowd.

Stay in line. Don't allow yourself to be vulnerable to rejection. You are not good enough to be successful. You don't deserve recognition. Your ideas are garbage.

If you knew anyone else that talked to you like this, you wouldn't invite them over to your house for drinks often. Yet, we live with this voice embedded in our minds every waking hour of every day of our lives. The demon is a relic of our prehistoric ancestors whose survival relied on this strategy: to go with the flow, follow the pack, and keep your head down. Today, this demon is an existential threat to our actualization as human beings. Learning to deal with and overcome this threat is an essential life skill that is unlikely to be found in the curriculum of your formal education. Further, to my knowledge, there is no eliminating this demon; there are only strategies for dealing with him.

I have spent my entire adult life sparring with this demon. I've tried various forms of meditation, therapy, and medication. I've found some relief and some success in each of those efforts. However, I have found one strategy to be more effective than the others. It is simple. It is cheap. In some ways, it is silly. But I have found it powerful enough to share it with you. The strategy is to allow yourself to suck. Yep. That's it. Give yourself permission to suck. It's more tactical than strategic, but it works for me.

As an example, as I am writing this book, my demon is relentless.

A book to your son? What could you possibly have to say that would be worth reading? Your life has been a series of failures. Is that what you want to teach Hunter—how to fail? Even if you had something to say that was worth reading, you are a horrible writer with no sense of style or flow. There are hundreds of books that Hunter can read written by people of purpose, insight, and wisdom. Why confuse him with your meaningless drivel? By the way, when will you find the time to write this great book of yours? Give it up before you embarrass yourself.

These thoughts bounce around my brain like an echo chamber. To be blunt, it is flat-out painful. In response to pain, we are hardwired to take action to make the pain go away. The easiest way to make the pain stop, to turn down the volume of the demon's taunts, is to give in to the demon.

Yes, you are right. I don't have anything of value to share. I am a terrible writer. I don't know what I was thinking. I give up. You win.

The demon wins. His voice subsides temporarily. The pain goes away. This book is never written. Although this response eliminates the immediate sharp pain of the demon's haunting, it contributes to a dull ache in the heart that comes from giving up on your dreams that intensifies each time the demon wins.

There is a form of martial arts called Judo (Japanese for the "gentle way") that focuses on how to use your opponent's weight, strength, and momentum against him, while preserving your own mental and physical energy. My strategy of allowing myself to suck reminds me of this.

Simply put-agree with the demon but do the work anyway. As you read this sentence, you have no idea what my demon is or isn't saying to me as I was writing it. More important than my self-talk at that moment is that the sentence was written, you are reading it, and my demon loses. However, I couldn't write that sentence and fight my demon at the same time. I just can't. I don't have that type of mental strength. So, I don't. I agree with the demon and give myself permission to suck.

Yes, you are right. I have nothing worth sharing or writing. I am a terrible writer. I'll never finish even if I do start it. But . . . I am going to write today anyway. I am going to write the worst drivel that I can muster. I'm not trying to prove you wrong. You'll see—it will be garbage. It will make for a good laugh. But . . . I am going to write today anyway.

It is tough to trick our minds like this, but I have found that it can be done. Today, as I write this letter, the only way that I was able to get my fingers to move on the keyboard and get words onto the screen was to truly "let myself suck." Sometimes, I actually pretend that I am playing a part in a movie. My character is a horrible writer but loves to write anyway. Then I give myself permission to be that character. I distance myself from the quality of the output and just focus on doing the work. All the while, the demon is whispering in my ear—I know what you are doing. This isn't going to work. You can't fool me. In response, I figuratively nod my head in agreement. You are right. You are right. You are right. But . . . I am going to write today anyway.

I've used this strategy over and again in my lifetime. Fortunately, I have found that when I use this strategy it is only a matter of time before a miracle occurs. Yes, a miracle! Like Dorothy's house falling on the Wicked Witch of the West, a new character emerges in the plot. A new voice can be heard at a volume that competes with and then overtakes the demon. This sleeping giant's voice is filled with optimism and encouragement.

*You can do this! You were born to do this! Don't listen to the demon. Keep going. You're doing great!*

If you are reading this, it is because of this sleeping giant's voice. Unfortunately, the demon's voice is never silenced. Even when operating in the flow of the sleeping giant's encouragement, the demon gets his voice heard from time to time, but his power is diminished once the sleeping giant awakens!

There may be other ways to awaken the sleeping giant, but I found fighting the demon with mental Judo to be the most effective. Another way to look at this phenomenon is to realize that action does not follow motivation. Many people wait to feel motivated before taking action. This is a losing strategy. Action and action alone awakens the voice of our motivated and positive self. The results are compounding. The more action we take towards achieving our goals, the more motivated we feel, and the more motivated we feel, the more action we take. The real barrier is overcoming the inertia of inaction. It is in this realm where the demon's voice is the loudest and most painful.

Most importantly, please know that your demon is wrong. It is always wrong. No matter how dark the days may become, no matter how loud the demon may scream, and no matter how much you feel the pressure to give in to the demon—your demon is always wrong. Please never forget this. I have spent too many precious days of my life convinced that there was truth in the demon's lies, and it would pain me deeply for you to do the same.

*Love,*
*Dad*

*Dear Hunter*

When I was in 7th grade, my dad asked me if I wanted to go to the high school basketball courts for a game of one-on-one. It had been nearly a year since we last battled it out on the court. Since then, I had shot up to a height equal to his, and I was enjoying a tremendous amount of success on the local CYO basketball team. My confidence was at an all-time high. I was hopeful that this would be the day when I finally beat my dad in a game of one-on-one. I laced up my brand-new Air Jordan high-top basketball sneakers and headed to the courts with a pep in my step.

On this rainy and cold morning in late November, my spirits went from hopeful to crushed in less than an hour. My dad wiped the court with me. The game wasn't even close. To my dismay, my fancy new Air Jordan basketball sneakers were more of an indoor sneaker. I was slipping and sliding all over the court. My dad was scoring point after point, and I was on my ass more than I was on my feet. I vividly remember complaining, "I can't stop slipping." My complaints fell on deaf ears as my father's $15 tennis shoes seemed to serve him just fine on the wet court. I recall being thankful that it was raining because the raindrops hid the tears streaming down my cheeks. I was frustrated beyond description. My dad made no allowance for my circumstance. "Stop complaining and play ball."

The moral of this story took several decades for me to grasp— anticipate your sneakers being slippery. Stop complaining and play ball.

Stay with me.

Nearly 30 years later, I was the keynote speaker for an Operational Excellence conference in Orlando, Florida. I had been doing a fair amount of public speaking in those days, but this would be my largest audience yet—about 3,000 people. I was a bit nervous but had grown very confident in my public speaking abilities. I had completed all my pre-talk rituals (reviewing my presentation, walking the space, talking to the audio/visual folks, etc.). Within seconds of beginning my presentation, I was stunned. The lights were so bright that I couldn't see the audience. Additionally, the audio was different than I had grown accustomed to so I couldn't hear myself. I was blind and deaf. A large part of my modest success as a public speaker was my ability to engage the audience. Without being able to see the audience, I found connecting with them nearly impossible. I was a rudderless ship. I was frustrated and embarrassed. I was bombing. Then I had a flashback to the cold and rainy November morning of 1987 when my dad told me, "Stop complaining and play ball." A response that I considered cruel and heartless decades ago was what I needed to pull me out of this tailspin. I mustered all the confidence and positivity that I could. I reminded myself to trust my content and trust in my abilities. Pull yourself together. I finished the presentation, and although it was not my finest moment, it certainly wasn't my worst. More importantly, the moral of the basketball story crystallized in my mind.

Anticipate your sneakers being slippery. Stop complaining and play ball.

One of my favorite expressions is, "If you want to make God chuckle, tell Him about your plans." Life has a funny way of humbling us. Predictably so. There will always be variables beyond our control that we must contend with. Always. It does us no good to lament the existence of these variables, or complain about them, or allow them to defeat us. They are part of life. There is no way of negotiating life's peculiar ways of humbling us. Accept and embrace them as they come and go. Like the weather, they are beyond your control.

Random and uncontrollable variables will arise in all facets of your life. You are at a baseball game, and the drunk guy behind you spills his beer on your shirt. You return to your car in the grocery store parking lot, and you find someone has scratched your car. There is a question on your exam on a subject that the professor didn't cover. Your boss blames you for something that you didn't do. The list will be endless. Life is full of slippery sneakers and blinding lights.

I recall a plaque that my grandparents had in their kitchen that profoundly impacted my life. It was the Serenity Prayer:

GOD, GRANT ME THE SERENITY TO ACCEPT
THE THINGS I CANNOT CHANGE,

COURAGE TO CHANGE THE THINGS I CAN,

AND THE WISDOM TO KNOW THE DIFFERENCE.

The simplicity of the Serenity Prayer belies its powerful message. The message relates to the expectation of control that we have over our life. My heart goes out to people who are sometimes referred to as "control freaks." Most suffering in life can be attributed to a state of existence where our expectations do not match reality. Because of this fact, control freaks are in a near-constant state of suffering because they have rigid expectations for nearly everything. I've learned that one of the keys to happiness in life is to reduce your expectations to a bare minimum. Doing so is not the equivalent of diminishing your hopes, dreams, and ambitions. Instead, it is a recognition that the universe is full of disorder and chaos so, therefore, we shouldn't expect our lives to be absent of disorder and chaos. Our minds do not like this notion. Our minds seek order and predictable patterns. We can, and must, train our brains to not only expect the unexpected but to accept the unexpected. I'll take it a step further and say that we should strive not only to accept the unforeseen but to embrace it. Often, amid uncertainty is where our most incredible opportunities lie.

Here's an example. After retiring from the United States Navy, I remained in Hawaii and launched my civilian career. I accepted a position at an industrial park in Honolulu to run their facilities as the Vice President of Operations. The industrial park had been developed, constructed, and run by a gentleman who had recently passed away. His son and daughter inherited the operation but lived in Seattle. The organization was woefully mismanaged, but I was thankful for the opportunity to sink my teeth into this turnaround assignment. My first seven months were terrific. I received nothing but accolades from the brother and sister, I was well-liked by the staff, and my leadership efforts were beginning to show substantial operational and financial results. In fact, the brother and sister were having discussions with me about other long-term opportunities in their company. Then— boom! — Like a pair of slippery sneakers or blinding lights, I was asked to resign. No reason. No discussion. Nothing. It was the first time in my life when I had felt that my professional efforts had fallen short. I had failed, and worse—I had no idea why. After licking my wounds under a blanket on the couch for a few days, I decided it was time for me to leave the island of Oahu and return to the mainland. I was now unemployed and uncertain about my professional future. Where would I find a job? Doing what? When? I had moments of resolve and moments of doubt but make no mistake; this was a chapter of chaos and disorder in my life. However . . .

The two-month-long job search that followed led me to a job in Kansas City, which then led me to Chicago. In Chicago, I fell in love with your mother. Shortly afterwards, you came along. I can trace the two most beautiful things in my life back to a moment of uncertainty, chaos, and disorder. Although I could not have predicted such a stroke of fortune, I like to think that my willingness and ability to remain open to life's possibilities gave me the courage and strength to find your mother amid a tumultuous time of my life.

My son, please learn to stay open to life's possibilities and opportunities even when faced with disappointment and pain. You truly never know what is waiting for you around the corner. Further, please remember slippery sneakers and blinding lights are neither good nor bad—they just are. Please learn to treat them with an open and curious mind. You can't control them, so it is best to learn how to embrace them.

*Love,*
*Dad*

*Dear Hunter*

John Lennon once said, "Life is what happens to you while you're busy making other plans." When I first heard this saying, I was 19 years old with no real-world experiences to speak of, but, for some reason, that quote resonated deeply with me. I interpreted it as a warning against allowing life to pass me by. Decades later this saying still profoundly resonates with me, but now I view the adage as less of a warning and more as a poignant observation. I'm not going to stop making plans for my life, for my family, for my hopes, and for my dreams. However, knowing that each passing moment of life IS life allows me to be more present and mindful.

As a freshman in college, my roommate introduced me to two books by Dan Millman titled, Way of the Peaceful Warrior, and No Ordinary Moments. The books blew my mind. It was the first time I had read a book that examined and explored how to live life in a meaningful way. The books chronicled the fictional relationship and conversations between an ordinary college student and an older and spiritually enlightened gas station attendant. Their relationship was Luke Skywalker and Yoda-esque, minus the light sabers and levitation. In No Ordinary Moments, the mentor instructs the mentee to retreat in solitude and meditate until he uncovers a cathartic universal truth. Ultimately, the mentee concludes that there are no ordinary moments in life. In their discussion of this philosophical reveal, they develop a mantra—the wisest answers to the questions, "What time is it?" and "Where are we?" are "Now" and "Here," respectively. When I am anxious, I often repeat this to myself over and over again.

What time is it? Now. Where am I? Here.

In various stages of my life, I've had to remind myself that every moment is unique and powerful. Upon further contemplation, I've concluded that the present moment is all we have in this life that is real. The past and future do not exist; they are mere shadows and estimations of reality. Before you dismiss that last sentence as philosophical nonsense, please take a moment to consider a few things. As a moment passes, it is truly gone. There is no going back. All that remains is a memory of the moment. That memory "exists" only as an electrical impulse in the brain. Nowhere else. Further, no two people's memories of an event are the same. Memories are not historically accurate. They exist in the context of our emotions, perceptions, and biases. The past, on a moment-to-moment basis, becomes but a shadow of reality. The future exists even less, in any real sense. You will likely often find your mind worried about the future. What if this happens? What if that happens? There is nothing wrong with considering your future as you make life decisions, but resist trading your peace and happiness at this moment for a future that is a mere figment of your imagination. As Mark Twain once quipped, "I've lived through some terrible things in my life, some of which actually happened."

One of the most challenging times of my life was my last nuclear submarine deployment in the United States Navy. The year was 2007. I was a Lieutenant Commander and the Chief Engineer aboard a nuclear submarine, the USS Key West (SSN-722) stationed in Pearl Harbor, Hawaii. The deployment was scheduled to be seven months long. Seven months is a long time to be away from home, friends, and family. It is an exceedingly long time to be cooped up in a tin can with 150 other people. By this time in my career, I had grown accustomed to the discomfort and challenges that submarine deployments present, but this deployment challenged my endurance and mental stamina. The missions we were assigned were the most daunting of my career. Additionally, I found the culture aboard that ship to be toxic. Don't get me wrong; I was surrounded by outstanding people, many of whom I remain friends with to this day.

However, I found the command element of that submarine to be severely lacking in necessary leadership skills. I'll save the details for another day. Suffice to say, I was miserable for the first and only time in my naval career. The experience was as close to prison as I hope I will ever experience.

I distinctly remember laying in my rack only several days into the deployment thinking, "How will I ever survive seven months of this?" I have never felt so helpless and hopeless. It was then when I realized the flip side of what I previously had considered the greatest tragedy of life. Specifically, the passage of time is relentless. There is no stopping time. There is no slowing time down. Time waits for no man. In a dark and hopeless chapter of my life, I rediscovered the beauty of an age-old expression — "This too shall pass." I wasn't serving a life sentence. My current situation was temporary. I would live to recollect these days and these feelings. In all likelihood, I would be mentally tougher as a result of the experience.

This perspective helped, but it proved insufficient to get me through the days that lay ahead. A few days later, I found myself contemplating the same thoughts of hopelessness and helplessness. This time, I decided to shift my focus on the rest of the crew. As Chief Engineer, nearly half of the ship reported to me. I thought about these 60 men. Were they laying in their racks with similar thoughts? If I was experiencing these feelings, so must they also be. As a leader, I owed them my best effort to improve their quality of life. I wanted to show them my best side, not my worst side. Could I inspire them? Could I comfort them? Could I help them deal with some of their feelings that may be similar to mine? I resolved that not only could I do this, I must do this. It was my duty. Feeling sorry for myself was a loser's strategy, and I wasn't interested in being a loser.

This resolution to focus on other people served me well, for a time. But eventually, I was still back to wallowing in my misery. I just didn't see how I could possibly get through this deployment. I felt like the enemy was my chain of command. Every step I took in carrying out my duties was met with an equal and opposite step to thwart my efforts. I know well that there are two sides to every story, and you are only hearing my side, but truth be told that is how I felt. As I dug deep into my toolbox of mental tricks, I discovered a tool that I had not previously used. As I tossed it around in my mind, I knew that I had found something special. I realized that I didn't have to finish the remaining six months of this deployment. I failed to apply the principles that I learned in my dorm room many moons ago while reading No Ordinary Moments. Life existed only one moment at a time, not six months at a time. I did not have to worry about finishing the remaining six months of this deployment; I had only to worry about the present moment. More pragmatically, I had only to worry about my next six-hour watch. I could do a six-hour watch as Officer of the Deck standing on my head. That was easy. It was the prospect of standing 240 more watches that had me worked up. I learned on that deployment to "shrink my time horizon." Instead of worrying about the 240 more watches in my future, I would focus my energy and attention on the only next one. I survived the deployment because of this focus. I never worried about next month or even tomorrow. I learned to embrace and confront only the moment that was right in front of me.

That submarine deployment taught me the magical triad of dealing with dark days that I hope you can use:

1. Remember—This too shall pass.

2. Focus on others.

3. Shrink your time horizon.

On my deployment, I felt that time couldn't pass fast enough. However, for most circumstances, the passage of time can be one of the great tragedies of our life if we don't condition ourselves to embrace what we have when we have it. We spend an excessive amount of our precious time and energy planning our future, or worse, waiting for our future. Meanwhile, time marches on, and life happens. The most common trap in life is lulling ourselves into delaying our happiness until X occurs — where X is a new stage of life, an achievement, a milestone, or a certain amount of money earned. There is only one appropriate time in our lives to seek happiness, and that time is NOW.

I have witnessed people who take this idea to a place that I don't want to see you go. Specifically, I am not encouraging you to live life with a philosophy that abandons investing in or sacrificing for your future. Your future self will thank you for your investments and sacrifices. It is wise and fulfilling to nurture your garden of hopes and dreams. However, the journey towards your hopes and dreams is every bit as precious as the achievement of those hopes and dreams. My experience is that the happiness that accompanies arriving at the destination of a goal pales in comparison to that which is achieved on the journey. Fall in love with the journey but only befriend the destination.

*Love,*
*Dad*

*Dear Hunter*

You make decisions all day long, every day, for your entire life. Right now, you've decided to read this sentence. You could have chosen to slam this book shut, hop on a cross-country train and join a travelling carnival. Here you are again. The decision train never stops—text, email, phone calls, conversations, events. One decision at a time, our future is molded. The most critical life skill is decision making because the consequences of our decisions ultimately define our lives.

Given the amount of practice we have in decision making, you'd think that we would be pretty darn good at it. If instead of making decisions all day long, you juggled all day long, you would, in time, be a world-class juggler. If practice were all that was required, everyone you know would be a world-class decision-maker. I don't believe this is the case. My observation is that people tend to struggle with decision making because they fail to reflect on their process and potential pitfalls. There are a lot of variables at play behind the scenes of even the simplest of decisions. Let's reflect.

Let's start our reflection with a look into the fundamental nature of decisions. Decisions are the choices we make based on the options available to us. What guides these decisions? Usually, but not always, it is our priorities. Our priorities shift from year to year, day to day, and even minute to minute. Our shifting priorities explain why we make different decisions across time and space in circumstances that may appear identical. We are not necessarily making a better or worse decision, just a different one because our priorities have shifted. Unfortunately, many people are unaware that their priorities are driving their choices. As a result, they may make their decisions haphazardly.

Set and own your priorities. Base your decisions on those priorities, and then accept the resulted outcome. If you eat lunch at McDonald's today, it is because your current priorities weigh convenience, speed, and price above health. Is that the right decision? That's not for me to answer. However, you should, from time to time, examine your priorities and ensure they are consistent with your vision for your future. If you want to become a neurosurgeon someday but you consistently prioritize playing video games over studying biology, you may want to spend some time reflecting on your priorities and aligning them with your vision for your future.

A human weakness that I have observed is that people tend to draw conclusions based on patterns derived from insufficient data, especially when our emotions are at play. A few years ago, I wrote an article with the hope of having it published. After the third rejection letter, I gave up. My ego was bruised, and I concluded that my writing sucked. There were hundreds of other publications to which I could have submitted this article. Was my decision to give up a rational decision? Of course not. Rejection hurts, and if you choose to avoid the possibility of further rejection by retreating into your shell, that's your decision. However, do not fool yourself and believe you are making a decision that serves your future well. In this case, my priority was to avoid the pain of rejection instead of prioritizing my future as a writer. As an aside, I can tell you that the sting of rejection pales in comparison to the weight of a dream unfulfilled.

Another Achilles heel in our decision-making instinct is that we are afraid of being wrong AND alone. Being wrong can be scary enough for some people but being wrong AND alone is too much to stomach for most. This is why financial bubbles happen. There is a saying about decision-makers that is both absolutely true and also impossible: "The majority of decision-makers will wait for the majority of decision-makers to do something before they will."

In the months leading up to the financial disaster of 2009, ample information was available to conclude that the housing market had grown out of control. Yet, the world's "wisest" investors continued to invest in residential real estate. Why? Presumably, because the majority of the other "wisest" investors continued to do so as well. We are susceptible to valuing the opinions of others above logic and reason.

I mentioned earlier in this letter that usually, but not always, our priorities are the driving factor behind our decisions. When priorities are not the driving factor, logic is. This is most applicable in more uncommon circumstances when the outcome of a decision at hand is binary: win or lose, right or wrong. Most of our decisions are much more nuanced, but it's worth discussing these black-and-white decisions. In these cases, do not assume that a good outcome means that you made the right decision.

Consider a hypothetical card game of blackjack where the objective is to get as close to 21 without going over. You receive a king and a queen for a hand of 20. The dealer has a 7 showing and another card face down. Should you "hit" and accept another card or "stick" and stay with your hand of 20? Let's assume you choose to "hit" and were dealt an ace for a perfect score of 21. You win! But did you make the right decision? Most card players would agree that you made an illogical decision but got lucky—which, by the way, is perfectly fine; we all deserve a dash of luck from time to time. However, I wouldn't recommend you believe that your decision was a good one. If you used this logic for an extended period, you would eventually lose all of your money to the house.

A powerful method for making difficult life decisions that align with your vision for the future is to listen to your "little man." I believe that we each have a gentle whispering voice inside of our mind (I choose to think of mine as coming from a little man) that exists precisely to help us make difficult life decisions. I know, I know; this is a very scientific method, right? Scientific or not, I've come to believe that this little voice is a rock star sage. It methodically and miraculously tracks, deconflicts, and weighs our future objectives and tells us what we should do in any given moment to optimize our chances of meeting these objectives. The challenge is drowning out the louder noise in our minds to hear this little voice. If there are times when you can't hear his whispering, it is not because the little man is on a coffee break. You can't hear him because your mind is too noisy. The most effective way to develop a reliable conduit between you and the little guy is by meditating and gaining life experiences. Even ten minutes of meditating is an incredibly effective way to hear this little voice. Experience is the way he gathers wisdom. Don't be afraid of making a poor decision. At worst, your little guy will have learned something. Some may be inclined to call this little voice our "gut instinct," and I would agree.

Notwithstanding the significance of healthy decision making to the quality of your life, I'd like to temper this message with a less stressful parting thought: Relax and don't take your decisions so seriously. Most decisions that you make do not carry substantial consequences. What color should we paint the bedroom? What should we have for dinner tonight? What movie should we watch? Not all decisions are created equal, so please don't treat them as if they are. I have observed that people experience excessive amounts of anxiety when they suffer through every decision placed in front of them. This can result in "decision fatigue" and is a consequence of over-analyzing every decision in your life. This is exhausting. Don't allow yourself to do this.

Further, learn to let go of your emotional attachment to the outcome once you make a decision. If your decision is irreversible, let it go like a helium balloon into the sky. Don't give it another thought and certainly do not second-guess yourself. It's wasted energy. Even if the decision proves to be one that you wouldn't make again, move on. You can't unmake that decision. Live to fight another day. Regardless of how much energy you put into your decisions, learn to accept that some decisions will result in a positive outcome, and some decisions will result in a negative or neutral outcome. Give yourself grace when evaluating the outcomes of your decisions. Perfection is unattainable.

*Love,*
*Dad*

*Dear Hunter*

Before heading off to my freshman year of college, I applied for a summer internship at the investment bank, Goldman Sachs. The company responded to my application with an in-person interview invitation at their New York City office. I dug up a suit and tie, likely the same one that wore to my high school prom, and I was off. I remember being excited and at ease as I navigated the city's subways during the morning rush hour. As my high school's valedictorian, a three-sport varsity athlete, and the recipient of a full academic scholarship to Rutgers University, I had grown to believe my own press. What I failed to consider was that I needed to prepare for the interview. I hadn't lifted a finger in preparation. As I entered the building at 200 West Street in New York's financial district, I was about to be introduced to the meaning behind the expression, "If you fail to prepare, prepare to fail."

To this day, memories of that interview conjure up feelings of inadequacy and shame within me. The gentleman who interviewed me is but a faceless suit in my memory. However, I remember the embarrassment that washed over me within the first 10 minutes of the interview. I don't recall the specific questions that I was asked, but I will never forget that I couldn't answer them in any meaningful way. I imagine they were basic questions: *"Why are you interested in this internship?" "What do you know about Goldman Sachs?" "What are your post-college career ambitions?"* I remember him telling me within 20 minutes that I would not be a good fit to intern at Goldman Sachs. Then, boom—back out onto the streets of New York City feeling discouraged and embarrassed. I remember chalking up the experience to a miscommunication with Goldman Sachs' human resource department. I fed my ego with all types of narratives to protect myself from the pain of the truth: *They were looking for someone older. They were looking for someone about to graduate college, not someone about to enter college. The man who interviewed me was a jerk. I don't want an internship this summer anyway.* The truth was that I was woefully unprepared, and it showed.

In addition to being unprepared, at that stage of my life and for many years after, I didn't grasp the purpose of the job application process. Our formal education system doesn't, in my opinion, assist in creating the right mindset for landing a job. I was encouraged by my schools, intentionally or not, to "collect" accomplishments. These accomplishments were, I believed, the keys to opening up the doors to the most prestigious colleges and professional opportunities. My college application process was all about "me"—what I had accomplished. This strategy may get you into Harvard, but it will not serve you well beyond the formal education system.

Why not?

Because the formal education system exists to support the students. Without students, there is no university. In most corporate organizations, the workers support the mission of the organization, not vice versa. This relationship requires a mindset reversal that some people never accomplish. Likely, no one will ever say or admit what I am about to tell you, but it's true. Ready? Interviewers do not care about your accomplishments. They may ask you about them. They may listen intently as you describe them. But . . . they don't care. Interviewers are evaluating you as you relate to the objectives of the organization. They are assessing if you will add value to the organization. Therefore, you must learn to frame your accomplishments in a way that conveys why you add value to the organization. This is true as it relates to academic, athletic, and professional accomplishments.

In addition to what you say about your accomplishments and achievements, consider your tone. I've interviewed hundreds of candidates for corporate positions. Most of them display their energy and enthusiasm when discussing themselves, but few match this energy when asking questions about the company or their possible role within the company. Don't get me wrong; it's okay to be proud about what you have achieved, but don't forget that the central character in this act of the play is the company and not you.

Whether you are 18 years old interviewing for a summer internship or 45 years old interviewing for a senior management position, interviewing can be uncomfortable and potentially nerve-racking. Here are some other interviewing tips that I have picked up along the way that may serve you well.

- Be you. Ultimately, an interview goes well because the people who interviewed you, liked you. I wish that I could tell you that the best person for the job always gets the job. I can't because that just isn't true. What is true is that the person that the interviewer liked the most usually gets the job. How do you increase your "likability"? The answer lies in the power of authenticity. You must be yourself. Displaying authenticity will not ensure that you get the job, but not being authentic will ensure that you don't get the job. I promise you. If the interviewer gets even a whiff that you are putting on a show or trying to be someone you are not, you will not get the job. It's that simple. If you follow one piece of advice in this letter, let it be this: Just be you!

- Manners matter. If I did my job raising you right, this should go without saying because manners ALWAYS matter, but if I failed to teach you this lesson, here are some basics. Arrive at the office—not the building, not the parking lot, but the office—where you are interviewing 10 minutes early. Say "please" and "thank you" to every person with whom you interact. Do not interrupt anyone while they are speaking. If you accept a bottle of water or a cup of coffee, do not leave your empty cup on the table. Ask where you can dispose of it. Sit up straight. Don't look at the clock. Maintain polite eye contact. Send everyone that you interviewed with a thank-you note within 24 hours of your interview. I have witnessed many qualified candidates fail to exhibit these basic displays of manners and weaken their employability.

- Be prepared, but resist the temptation to show off. Use the information that you researched naturally; don't force it. You should know the basics of the company that you would like to hire you. Examples of basics include when and where the company was founded, the major business lines the company is engaged in, and some basic financial data such as stock price, annual revenue, and annual profit. Familiarize yourself with any recent news about the company such as acquisitions or divestitures, new product lines, or new facilities.

- Answer questions clearly and concisely. Many people get very wordy when they get nervous. Be remembered as a candidate who was focused and succinct. I would prefer that you leave your interviewer wanting more from you rather than overstaying your welcome.

- Resist the temptation to speak negatively about a past or current employer. This can be tricky and challenging territory to navigate if you left a job because you were dissatisfied with the employer. However, there are no circumstances in which it is acceptable to speak ill of a previous employer—none. You can and should send the message by taking the high ground if asked why you left or why you want to leave a job: "I am extremely grateful for the opportunity to have worked with X company, but I am ready for a new challenge in a new environment." The interviewer will get the message, and you will avoid casting yourself in a negative light for bad-mouthing an employer.

- Don't take rejection personally. Inevitably, you will be over the moon enthusiastic about a particular job opportunity. You will be sure that the position is perfect for you and that you are perfect for the position. You will crush the interview and then wait for a job offer that never comes. This will happen. When it does, don't take it personally. The universe has an uncanny way of taking care of us. Although you may not understand it, there is a good reason why you didn't get that job. Let it go into the sky like a helium balloon, and then move on with your life.

*Love,*
*Dad*

*Dear Hunter*

The French novelist, Gustave Flaubert, once said, "Be regular and orderly in your life, so that you may be violent and original in your work." Stated less eloquently, our mental and physical resources are limited. Therefore, optimize the resources you have for the work that requires them by minimizing the resources applied to lower priority work.

Cultivate habits that help you make the routine things in your life genuinely routine. If you do so, you free up immeasurable mental bandwidth that you can use on less routine and more significant endeavors. Please note, I am not talking exclusively about saving time. I am talking about the mental reserves that you consume every time you have to make a decision or attend to an issue in your life. For example, consider your clothes for a moment. One of the daily routines that I miss the most about my United States Navy career is putting on my uniform. I was always thankful that I never had to consider what I was going to wear. In the same way, when at sea; I was grateful for the meals prepared for the crew by the cooks. All I had to do was show up and eat without making any decisions. I had plenty of decisions to make each day, and my clothes and food represented daily tasks where my mind could rest. I'm not the only one who appreciates this approach. President Barack Obama once said, "You'll see I wear only gray or blue suits. I'm trying to pare down decisions. I don't want to make decisions about what I'm eating or wearing because I have too many other decisions to make." Steve Jobs and Albert Einstein were also known for subscribing to this philosophy. Studies have shown that "decision fatigue" is real. More specifically, the quality of our decisions degrade as the quantity of our decisions increase.

One strategy that you can employ to help you keep your daily life regular and ordinary is to look for opportunities to reduce the number of decisions you make in a day. For example, a person might assess how much money he can save each month. Doing so requires that person to make a decision and then act on that decision each and every month. Instead, that person can eliminate 11 decisions a year by making the financial assessment on an annual basis by determining how much money he wants to save each month and then setting up an automatic transfer of funds between his checking account and savings account. Aggressively look for opportunities to duplicate this process to other facets of your life. If you can make a habit of eliminating ordinary daily decisions, you will be rewarded with more mental bandwidth to use creatively in other areas of your life.

I'd encourage you to consider the number of decisions you make daily and the amount of effort you put into these decisions. Some things are more important than others, and your effort and attention should reflect this. Presently, I have three main priorities in my life: my family, my work, and my writing. I do my best to remind myself that any energy expended outside of these priorities is stealing from them. Of course, it is unreasonable to assume that 100 percent of my life is devoted to these three items; however, I feel compelled to maximize the amount of energy I commit to these priorities. Doing so often results in thoughts of inadequacy. My car isn't clean. I haven't played a round of golf in two years. I am not going to the gym. I am not staying in touch with friends. My closet is a mess. I am not reading as much as I used to. I am not working on my PhD. These thoughts are stressful and anxiety-inducing. I am reminded of some advice I heard years ago from a source I cannot recall: "You can have it all, but you can't have it all at the same time." Many people assume that they can tackle everything in their lives with an equal amount of vigor. These efforts are noble and valiant. However, it is my experience that these people always seem to be falling apart at the seams. Thinking that you can tackle everything in your life at the same time usually comes from a place of wanting to please everyone.

Please listen carefully, my son . . .

YOU CAN'T PLEASE EVERYONE.

I am NOT saying that you can't be empathetic, kind, and compassionate to everyone, but you will drive yourself crazy trying to please everyone. The sooner in life you accept this fact, the better. Trying to please everyone is a recipe for disaster. Truly. The harsh reality of this truism is that often the people you will not be able to satisfy are people you truly adore and admire, such as your friends, family, and co-workers. At my core, I am a people pleaser. I don't want to let anyone down or disappoint anyone. It gives me a sinking feeling in my stomach to even think about letting someone down. However, I have spent a great deal of effort training myself to learn a word that will rattle most people's cage. *No.* Sometimes you have to say *no. No, I can't go out tonight. No, I can't talk on the phone. No, I can't come to your party. No, I can't work on that project. No, I can't donate to that charity.* Learn to say *no* with humility, compassion, and grace, but learn to say *no.* You can. You will. You must. If you fail to learn this lesson, you will inevitably neglect the priorities in your life. Remember, each bit of energy devoted to something other than your priorities steals from the reserve that remains for your priorities.

Tangentially related to keeping your life "regular and ordinary" is one of my favorite quotes from Leonardo da Vinci, "Simplicity is the ultimate sophistication." When faced with options, always choose simple over complex—every single time. You know people, and you will meet more, who always seem to be overcome with drama in their lives. Chances are, these people are victims of the complexity bias. We all have tendencies to turn simple things into complex things, but the people that don't address this tendency are the ones who always seem to be fighting their way out of a spider's web of complexity.

The complexity bias is a fancy way of restating Confucius' observation that "life is really simple, but we insist on making it complicated." Complexity bias is our tendency to take something that is easy to understand and view it as having many components that are difficult to understand. Studies have shown that when people are presented with two competing hypotheses, one simple and one complex, they routinely select the more complex one as more likely to be true. Odd, huh? The complexity bias is considered a cognitive bias. And, like most cognitive biases, the tendency allows the brain to be lazy. Unconsciously, we choose to believe the answers to our problems are complex rather than simple because it obviates the need for us to understand the problem. If we don't understand the problem, we are less likely to feel responsible for solving the problem. In the fight-flight-freeze instinct of humans, the complexity bias represents the "flight." Consider Einstein's breakthrough concept of $E=mc^2$. Could the relationship between energy and matter be any simpler? Often, it is very challenging to derive simple solutions to complex problems, but it is genuinely remarkable how often this is the winning strategy.

Once we recognize our susceptibility to the complexity bias, we can embrace its converse— "Occam's razor." Occam's razor is the principle that "entities should not be multiplied without necessity." More plainly, the simplest explanation is usually the right one. Once armed with the acceptance of Occam's razor and an awareness of the complexity bias, we open ourselves to relief and a life-changing peace. However, embracing this concept takes practice and energy because solutions should be as simple as possible, but no simpler. Recall, the complexity bias is considered a cognitive shortcut because it removes the necessity for us to determine the real cause of our problems. Once this shortcut is removed, we are left with the realization that the solutions to most of our problems are in the palm of our hand. Our responsibility and duty are to act upon them.

*Love,*
*Dad*

*Dear Hunter*

You will, if you haven't already, be blessed with the opportunity to lead others. Being a "leader" is fulfilling and extraordinary. You have the opportunity to improve the lives of the people you lead by inspiring and motivating them to achieve what they previously did not believe was possible. Being a successful leader requires that you understand that the groups you lead are composed of diverse personalities.

Consider a hypothetical morning staff meeting. As you scan the room and look at your staff, you see individuals. These individuals have unique dominant personality traits—self-motivated, ambitious, lazy, bitter, "all talk and no action," introspective, procrastinating, underperforming, over performing, indifferent, domineering, comedic, dependable, loyal, and unpredictable. This cast of characters looks to you for "leadership"—but that "leadership" means something different to each of them, and it is your job to deliver.

Your success as a leader is largely dependent on your ability to apply different leadership techniques to different personality types at different times in different contexts. Few would agree that one-size leadership fits all. Leadership styles that excel with some personalities fail miserably with others. I like to think of leadership similarly to the way I think about light. If someone asked you, "What makes a good light?", your answer would likely be, "It depends on the circumstance." A lamp, a floodlight, a flashlight, a candle—these are all effective lights for the right circumstance. A lamp makes a good light for reading a book, but it isn't a good light for searching your backyard at night for an intruder.

The same applies to being a good leader. If you try to squeeze the maximum productivity out of your "lazy" employee by treating him the same as your self-motivated employee, you will likely demotivate both. Further, telling a bitter employee to "stop being bitter" or a procrastinating employee to "stop procrastinating" will work as well as telling your dog to "stop being a dog." Effective leadership requires creativity, determination, and perseverance.

Before you can effectively lead others in such a dynamic and nuanced capacity, you must be able to lead yourself. Sounds easy. It is not. I'd like to share a thought experiment with you that may seem a bit silly on the surface, but it has served me well in leading myself through some troubled times. You have likely heard of the psychological disorder, multiple personality disorder (MPD). This term is applied to a person whose core personality changes frequently. These different personalities have different names, backstories, ages, genders, speech patterns, and beliefs. From what I understand and imagine, this disorder is debilitating. Individuals who suffer from MPD often cannot function in our society. This is true in its extreme form; however, I would contend that we all suffer from a very mild form of MPD.

The milder form of this disorder is most evident when you commit to a change in lifestyle or habit. Imagine that you are motivated to eat healthier and exercise regularly. You establish a new diet and workout routine. A few weeks later, who is the creature lying on the couch with a bag of Doritos on his chest watching Seinfeld reruns during designated gym time on Wednesday? Is this the same person who committed to a new lifestyle? Is this "you"? Are "you" dedicated to this new routine or are "you" not? What explains our Jekyll-and-Hyde tendencies? I present for your consideration a tongue-in-cheek answer—our multiple personalities.

So how do we lead this group of characters that inhabit the same mind? The most common tool used to deal with this challenge is the same tool that we earlier agreed would never work. We tell our lazy personality, "Don't be lazy." We tell our pessimistic personality, "Don't be pessimistic." When this strategy doesn't work when dealing with others, we have the option of terminating their employment or walking away from a toxic person. Do we have that option within ourselves? Can we fire our lazy personality? I have found this impossible. We can strengthen the other personalities through cultivating habits that minimize the appearance of the unproductive personalities, but we can't eliminate them.

Leading your many "selves" is much trickier than leading a group of people with diverse personalities because we have less control over what character we will have to deal with at any given time. When our lazy self shows up, he takes over and we're stuck with him for a while. When that happens, is it unreasonable to call this internal character into the office of your mind for counselling sessions? When dealing with others, we know that a calm and professional discussion that is proactive, compassionate, and strategic is always more fruitful than discussions that are reactive, emotional, and off-the-cuff. Why would it be any different with your own personalities? What if you spent some time discussing your expectations with each of your personalities proactively?

Imagine calling one of your in-need-of-fixing personalities into your mind's office for a heart-to-heart discussion. You could express your expectations and your empathy. You could say to Mr. Lazy that vegging on the couch and binge-watching television shows for hours on end is damaging the "company," while also expressing your understanding of why he does it. Perhaps, if you put your heads together, you could identify a solution that allows television time, without wreaking havoc on your productivity. Imagine repeating this process with each of your personalities. I've beat up on Mr. Lazy as an example, but you know there are plenty of other personalities for you to meet. Also, let's not forget the positive personalities. Express your gratitude and then brainstorm how to see more of them consistently. Sometimes, it's good to brainstorm with these personalities about your "company's" goals and how best to achieve them, especially considering the existence and presence of some of the negative personalities.

Reasoning with your unproductive selves can be an effective strategy to make peace with them. Negotiating with Mr. Lazy is okay, in my book. However, you don't negotiate with terrorists, and we all have darker sides that aren't interested in making peace. These demons rear their ugly heads from time to time—anger, hate, jealousy, greed, to name a few. For these characters, I recommend a different strategy. It reminds me of the fable of unknown origin where a grandfather tells his grandson, "Two wolves are fighting inside of you, an evil one and a good one." His grandson asks, "Who will win?" The grandfather replies, "The one you feed." You feed your good selves by cultivating the garden of your mind. Each thought represents habitation in your mind's garden. What do you do with the weeds? You eliminate them immediately. You certainly don't water them. I'd be lying if I told you that I've never watered the weeds in my mind's garden. Doing so is a temptation that requires years of practice to eliminate. Allowing these demons to plant their seeds in your mind's garden is self-sabotaging behavior. Buddha said, "Holding on to anger is like grasping a hot coal with the intent of harming another; you end up getting burned."

I haven't spoken to a very dear friend of mine from high school in nearly 30 years because I chose to feed the wrong wolf. This friend and I had known each other since kindergarten and became romantically linked towards the end of high school. We were never destined to be more than friends, but I chose to cut off all ties with her because of a perceived slight. As a result, I lost a very dear friend. Who was I punishing? When I held on to that anger for years, I convinced myself that I removed a toxic person from my life, but I never really believed that. The truth was that I was grasping a lump of hot coal while feeding the wrong wolf.

We all have multiple personalities that dwell in our minds. The key is strengthening the ones that you want to see more of and weakening the ones that you could live without. However, at the helm of this ship with multiple passengers is you. You are the captain of your ship and like a captain at sea, the responsibility and accountability of managing your people rests squarely on your shoulders. Develop the sense of when you need to be gentle with yourself and when you need to tighten the screws.

*Love,*
*Dad*

*Dear Hunter*

As an enlisted sailor in the United States Navy, I attended an Electronics Technician school in Orlando, Florida. The school was six months long and was for sailors who were selected to become reactor operators for nuclear submarines. This school was the first in a series of schools that I would attend before being certified as a reactor operator. The training pipeline for nuclear reactor operators is among the most arduous in the military. I had heard rumors about the low graduation rate. The stories were true. There were twenty-three sailors in my Electronics Technician class and only seven graduated. The Navy devotes many resources to pre-screening candidates before attending this school so it may seem surprising that so few graduate. Academically, the school was challenging, but every person who began the training had the intellectual capability to graduate. The individuals who didn't graduate were all removed from the program for "character flaws."

The specific "flaws" were varied and included underage drinking, not completing or cheating on homework, not completing the required amount of mandatory study hours, basic military instruction failures, and physical fitness failures. There was virtually no due process or second chance for those that didn't make the cut. Admittedly, I was hesitant to go out to clubs or bars in Orlando for fear of getting caught in some trouble that might get me kicked out of the program. We were taught that character and integrity were crucial to the nuclear Navy and that any character flaw was unacceptable. The standard was unflinchingly rigid. Although I was more than happy to drink the Kool-Aid and toe the line, I never really understood the logic behind these standards.

Let me share a story that will shed some light on the high standards in the United States Navy nuclear submarine force.

United States Navy nuclear submarines undergo an annual inspection called an ORSE (Operational Reactor Safeguards Examination). These inspections are intense. The submarine crew spends months preparing for this three-day, at-sea inspection. I vividly recall my first experience of an ORSE. I was a young junior officer aboard the fast-attack nuclear submarine USS HAMPTON (SSN-767) in 1999 in Norfolk, Virginia. The submarine buzzed with an energy I had never felt before or since. The days were filled with record reviews, evaluated maintenance activities, written tests, oral examinations, and reactor casualty drills. During a routine inspection of the engine room, one of the inspectors found a small rubber ducky floating hidden in the evaporator's chemical feed tank.

The inspection team's response to finding a rubber ducky in a nuclear submarine engine room was predictably unpleasant, but the magnitude of the response stunned me. The senior member of the inspection team halted the inspection. The submarine's commanding officer and the senior member of the inspection team had a closed-door meeting that lasted an hour or more. This discovery adversely impacted the submarine's grade on the inspection. After the inspection, the commanding officer convened an investigation to determine who in the engineering department knew about the rubber ducky's existence. The individuals that were determined to know, or should have known, were disciplined. Ensign DiGeronimo's mind was blown. I couldn't believe that something as innocuous as a small rubber toy could result in such an adverse reaction.

What I didn't understand then, I know now.

Specifically, the lesson for me is about buffers. The United States Navy is entrusted to operate nuclear reactors in every major naval port in the country. The amount of public trust and confidence that is required to continue to run these reactors is substantial. Most nuclear power plants are located in rural areas because there is a perception, right or wrong, that no one wants a nuclear power plant in their backyard. The United States Navy cannot suffer a reactor accident— period. If it did and the public was exposed to even the smallest amount of radiation or contamination, the entire program's existence would be in jeopardy. The most likely cause of a potential reactor accident is human error. That is not to say that a material failure could not occur, but you can trust me when I tell you that these reactors are designed to the absolute highest standards of engineering excellence. The potential threat lies in human performance.

A surefire way to ensure that human performance never falters to a level that would allow a reactor accident to happen is to create a buffer. The standard of professionalism is set with a tremendously large cushion around the actual threat level. When the buffer is hit, the organization responds as though the system failed and corrects the system. In the rubber ducky case, the organization responded as though this small display of unprofessionalism was a failure of the submarine's command team to establish and enforce adequate standards of professionalism consistent with those required to maintain the public's safety and trust. Did the rubber ducky threaten the public's safety? Of course not. It presented no threat to the public, but the organization protects itself from an unacceptable consequence by responding adversely to the buffer being hit.

I have learned that we can successfully apply the philosophy of buffers to our personal and professional lives as well. I am currently the Plant General Manager of a manufacturing facility. As the leader of the facility, I have established guideposts for the team to follow. Those guideposts are safety, integrity and respect. If we honor these principles in all that we do, we will be rewarded with a safe, pleasant, and prosperous work environment.

Let's take a look at the integrity guidepost. A scenario that we must avoid is unscrupulous financial or operational behavior. Integrity is doing the right thing even when no one is watching. How do I enforce integrity standards at the plant to ensure we never even enter the zip code of unscrupulous behavior? I do this by establishing buffers. For example, I do not "time travel," and I don't allow any of my staff to "time travel." Time travelling is signing your name with a date that is not today's date. The administration of a manufacturing facility can be daunting. There are required inspections, audits, environmental reports, etc. Most of these requirements have an associated time requirement, such as reviewing all financial transactions quarterly or inspecting the boiler room monthly. Auditors will look at the records related to these requirements to ensure compliance. It is common in the industry to "time travel" by signing the completion of such documents with the date that meets the required periodicity versus the date of actual completion. I do not allow this. If our monthly inspection of the boiler room for December was completed on January 5th, we would date the inspection documentation for January 5th. I would rather accept the consequences of an auditor's findings than flex our integrity. We do the right thing, even when no one is watching.

To some, this standard of no "time travelling" may seem silly. After all, it's just a signature on a piece of paper. Is "time travelling" immoral? Would someone go to jail for doing so? Would someone lose their job? No, but it represents the buffer that we have to ensure that we never venture into dangerous terrain. We manage complex tasks and substantial financial operations daily, so isn't how we date our signatures trivial? From my perspective, the power of this buffer is in what the standard represents to the team. It is a daily decision that reminds each of us that we do the right things, the right way, all the time. Even when no one is watching.

You can, and should, establish buffers in your personal life to protect yourself from figurative reactor accidents. What you choose to protect yourself from is a personal decision, and I'll leave that for you to decide, but know that buffers are a very effective way to keep yourself honest and out of harm's way.

*Love,*
*Dad*

*Dear Hunter*

You were born into a world of complexity and chaos. You were born into a world that is still absorbing the consequences of a technology boom in the 1990s that was supposed to bring us closer together. In some ways, we are closer together, and in other ways, we have never been farther apart. It remains a beautiful world full of hope, optimism, and possibility, but also a world where uncertainty and change seem to be the only constants. I have no idea what the future holds for you and your generation. One thing is for sure, however, you have a lot of information to absorb. The complexity surrounding you increases daily, and it can be challenging to distinguish between what is complexity and what is chaos. With chaos, there are no patterns or underlying rhyme or reason; whereas with complexity the patterns are difficult to discern, but they are there.

An odd characteristic of the internet age is that everyone seems to have a need to express their opinion on everything. When scrolling through thousands of posts, one has to wonder how it is possible for so many people to know so much about the magnitude of issues that are on the table.

What do you think about global warming? How about immigration reform? Our criminal justice system? Nuclear power? Chinese-American international relations?

These are complex issues that very few of us have spent much time researching or learning about. Further, there may be an infinite number of answers to these increasingly complex questions. Yet, there seems to be intense pressure to select the "right" answer from a few available options. But how? As social creatures, we take our social cues from our peers, and if everyone else has an opinion on "everything," I guess I will too. I find this exhausting, unrealistic, and inauthentic.

A few years ago, I read the book *How to Live: Or A Life of Montaigne* by Sarah Bakewell. The book revealed the ways in which Renaissance writers were obsessed with the question "How should we live life?" The book's main focus, Michael Eyquem de Montaigne who was considered the first "modern" individual, was no exception. Reading about his discovery of skepticism, and more specifically Pyrrhonist skepticism, had an intellectually rejuvenating effect on me. I'll save you the history lesson of the philosophy of skepticism, but the bottom line can be expressed with this saying, "All I know is that I know nothing, and I'm not even sure about that."

This group of philosophers would often use a one-word response to questions—*epekho,* which is Greek for "I suspend judgment." I think we'd all reduce our stress levels if we weren't incessantly holding ourselves to an unobtainable standard of having an answer to everything. Instead, we should learn to feel comfortable saying "I don't know" or even *epekho—I suspend judgment.*

In 2010, President Barack Obama signed the Affordable Care Act into law. This act was a politically divisive modification of our country's healthcare system. People from both sides of the aisle were screaming for its passage or its rejection. My friends and family were split, with both sides spitting venom on social media. I recall having an "epekho" moment when I realized that I didn't know what to think. Who could argue, given the name of the legislation: Affordable Care Act? That sounded good, but what did the 1500 pages of the bill say? What was buried in the details beyond the sound-bite description that we had heard from the media? I didn't know because I hadn't read the bill, and I didn't intend to. When I expressed this hesitation to state an opinion on the subject to my friends, I could tell that I had confused them. *What do you mean you don't have an opinion? Everybody does. It is the hottest topic in the news.*

While I'm not suggesting that you can only have an opinion on topics that you research extensively, I would encourage you to temper your tendency to take a hardline stance on a topic that you know only a little bit about. It's tempting, for sure. You will witness other people digging in their heels on every topic under the sun. Sometimes casual debate is recreational and harmless. However, train your mind to respect the words of Stephen Hawking who said, "The greatest enemy of knowledge is not ignorance, it is the illusion of knowledge."

Extend this further, as the Renaissance philosophers did, to our reactions to events in our lives. We are obsessed with categorizing events, moment by moment, as "good" or "bad." We have no idea whether being laid off from our jobs is "good" or "bad"—time will tell a story that is guaranteed to be vastly different than the one in your head today. You know this. The consequences of the events in our lives—caught in traffic, late for an appointment, underperforming during a presentation, closing the deal, receiving (or not receiving) the promotion—are rarely apparent to us at the moment they occur.

Might it be refreshing to try to react with "epekho" in response to your day's events?

I'm not sure we realize the damage we are doing to our psyche when we hold ourselves to an omnipotent standard. I challenge you, for just one day, to "suspend judgment" . . . take the weight off of your shoulders, let the universe unfold as it should and reveal the consequences to you. We are not the judge and jury of every detail of our lives, so why do we burden ourselves with the weight of that illusionary responsibility? And we certainly don't have to be an expert on the world's most complex and pressing issues. Keep in mind, I'm not suggesting that you shouldn't have an opinion; I'm merely reminding you that it is not necessary at all times. You can be very informed and still invoke the practice of *epekho*.

Try this for a day. Tell yourself, "I don't know" . . . "I'm not sure" . . . "I guess we'll see" . . . "I can't wait to see how this plays out." Take off the shackles of the obsessive need to categorize every minute detail of your life into categories of "good" and "bad."

Tangentially related is the topic of open-mindedness. Sometimes, you will have strong opinions. This is healthy and normal. *Epekho* represents a philosophy that reminds us that it is okay to reserve judgment on issues or events. However, you will pass judgment on topics when you feel comfortable in doing so. This is natural, but I would encourage you to keep at least a portion of your mind open to the possibility that you are wrong. Even the ideas and ideals that you hold most dear are subject to change. The people with the strongest minds that I know keep themselves open to this possibility.

We are imperfect beings. We know this, but how often do we make allowance for our imperfections? For example, just beneath our consciousness level, our brains interpret information to support our existing beliefs. This process is illogical yet true and supports Mark Twain's observation that it is easier to fool people than convince them that they have been fooled.

Yogi Berra once said, "In theory there is no difference between theory and practice. In practice there is." In theory, our brains would process information objectively so that our existing beliefs would be validated or adjusted based on the receipt of new information. In practice, we dismiss information that challenges our beliefs, embrace information that supports our beliefs, and relax our critical thinking when new but uncertain information is received.

More plainly, we see what we want to see. As a result, our thoughts are not nearly as critical as we convince ourselves they are. If our thoughts are the product of subpar analysis, and our thoughts shape our world, then there must be a substantial difference between our perception of the world and reality.

Our brains are wired to choose consistency over truth. Is that what you desire? If so, let your brain do its thing. If not, you must work to overcome this overwhelmingly powerful tendency. I challenge you to spend an hour, a day, or a week challenging a belief of yours. This could be something simple and personal like, "My boss doesn't like me." Or it could be something more complicated like, "The liberal media is ruining our country." What's the best way to challenge a belief? Embrace the contrary position. For the sake of the exercise, reevaluate your facts and try to get them to match the ideas that run counter to your own. Take notice of how your brain fights you during this experiment.

If you are feeling brave, try this exercise with an emotionally charged topic such as presidential candidates. Pick the candidate you disdain and try to convince yourself that this person is the country's best choice. This experiment is not unlike the scientific process. A theory is considered proven when it can't be disproven. Imagine it is the theory of your enemy that you desperately want to thwart. Look at the information from every angle you can and find a weakness, a crack, an overlooked exception, or a logic flaw.

As Aristotle once said, "It is the mark of an educated mind to be able to entertain a thought without accepting it."

*Love,*
*Dad*

*Dear Hunter*

A common motivational adage goes like this: "Success exists outside of your comfort zone." The model of success this adage implies is no exception to the truism that all models are wrong, and some are useful. More plainly, would I encourage you to see success as existing outside of your comfort zone? Yes and no.

Intuitively, we know that a comfort zone is an environment or situation where we feel content, secure, and relaxed. And naturally, we enjoy and seek out such environments and situations. But the mental construct of a singular comfort zone is restrictive and illogical. You don't have ONE comfort zone; you have many: at home with family or guests (two zones), at work with peers, clients, prospective clients, your boss (four more zones), skill sets such as public speaking, technical writing, negotiating, resolving conflict, managing teams, managing projects (another six). You build comfort zones as you gain experience in various environments. So, I don't want you to think about your "comfort zone" as a singular entity.

I contend that most success, in the traditional sense, exists only in a comfort zone. Success outside of a comfort zone is luck. I have no comfort with bullfighting; should I compete as a matador tonight and expect success? You don't scurry from the protection of a comfort zone to weather the elements like a wet rat and expect success for doing so. You build your comfort zones like real estate tycoons build developments. You then enjoy unimpeded access to and from these zones. Comfort zones are not the hiding places of the frail and feeble. They are the structures designed with your imagination, financed with your time, and constructed with your sweat.

If your existing comfort zones bear fruit that fulfils you—enjoy this comfort without feeling that you should "leave your comfort zone." After all, comfort is a luxury that we seek and not a status from which to escape. No motivational theory should attempt to shame you into believing that you have a personality flaw if you stay in your comfort zone. You are content for a reason. *If it's not broke, don't fix it.* However, if you are dissatisfied with your personal or professional life, selecting and constructing a new comfort zone may be a viable option. When you build new comfort zones, you expand your horizons—and the universe opens portions of itself that are closed to the general public. However, there is no award for the person who achieves the most expansive horizon.

Always build new comfort zones based on a thoughtful, deliberate, and measured process that serves your life priorities. I emphasize this because we live in a world that relentlessly shoves the "more is better than less" adage down our throats. I have more often found the opposite to be true. You only have 168 hours in a week. The decision on how to spend those hours—enjoying your existing comfort zones or building new ones—will ultimately define you and your legacy.

With all of that said, and at the risk of contradicting myself, I encourage you to develop the courage to operate outside of your comfort zone. I stand by my premise that success comes from operating inside your carefully constructed comfort zones. But I'd like to remind you that when you are operating in a comfort zone, stagnation, mediocrity, and complacency traps await. To avoid these traps, I encourage you to challenge yourself from time to time by exploring the world outside of your comfort zones, without assuming that is where success lies.

As a young officer in the United States Navy, I recall a senior officer remarking that the comfortable areas of a submarine should be labelled as "No Learning Zones." Learning the operation and workings of a nuclear submarine is an arduous journey. As a young, unqualified officer, I spent my days and nights studying the intricate details of this 6,900-ton war machine. The only spaces that I would consider "comfortable" for a young junior officer aboard a nuclear submarine are the wardroom (a space where officers eat, relax, and study) and the staterooms (spaces where officers sleep). These are the only places with desks or tables where one could sit and study in a familiar and comfortable way. I was perplexed and frustrated when this senior officer insisted that I study in the torpedo room or the engine room's lower levels. In these places, I would balance myself atop a valve or pipe while awkwardly holding six-inch thick technical manuals in my arms. The physical challenges of this setup were not trivial, but the mental challenges were even more significant. It was no easy task to study the principles of nuclear fission or the intricate workings of an ADCAP torpedo while trying to block out the noise of 3000-pound hydraulic pumps while fighting the nausea that comes from reading technical manuals in the bowels of the ship, while, at the same time, trying to ignore the mechanics who work in that space and found it entertaining to distract me with various shenanigans.

I was sure that the effectiveness of my studying was reduced because of this senior officer's hair-brained notion that I should study only in uncomfortable locations aboard the submarine. However, in time, I learned a few things by being forced to study in this manner. I learned that there is real value in learning how to be uncomfortable. On a submarine, and in life, being uncomfortable is commonplace. The varieties of discomfort are many: being tired, being hungry, being physically cramped, being distracted, being intimidated. Being able to perform your duties while being uncomfortable is critical to the submarine's safety and success. I am not recommending that you seek out discomfort; however, I encourage you to train yourself to accept discomfort when you must. Even if you pursue activities less prone to discomfort than serving on a submarine, I assure you that you will find that most people struggle to keep their wits about them when they are uncomfortable. Learn to do so.

Often, ventures outside of your comfort zones will not result in success by the most conventional definitions, but they will always result in personal growth—which is arguably more important. When I retired from the United States Navy, I was a bit lost. I struggled with mental and physical health issues, and I wasn't sure what the next chapters of my life would look like. However, I did have an entrepreneurial itch that I needed to scratch. I chased that feeling and launched a mergers & acquisitions firm. Notwithstanding a master's degree in Business Administration from the University of Connecticut, I had no training or experience in this industry. I leapt from a place of comfort, the Navy, to a place of extreme discomfort.

There's a saying, "You don't know how well you can dance until someone is shooting at your feet." I found myself dancing as an entrepreneur who had bills to pay and payroll to meet. I was completely over my head at times but learned to live with the discomfort of uncertainty. I was uncertain that I could make a living running a business in an industry where I had no experience. I was unsure what my next paycheck would look like, or if there would even be one. The business itself was modestly successful, and I exited that industry two years after entering it. Besides the business and financial acumen that I gained, I learned something about building comfort zones. Specifically, I learned about me. With no safety net or support structures in place, I came face to face, for the first time in my life, with the real me—warts and all. That view of myself was possible only because I left the cozy confines of my comfort zones. Having lived through that, I do not, as some do, recommend leaping out of an airplane and building the parachute on the way down. However, if you find yourself in that circumstance, I encourage you to use that time to get to know yourself because there is no better time to do so.

*Love,*
*Dad*

*Dear Hunter*

I would never pressure nor expect you to enter into military service. That choice is uniquely yours, and no one should attempt to sway you. You know that I did serve in the United States Navy, and although I am proud of my service, I expect nothing in return. My decision to serve our country in the military was a very personal one wrapped up in a lot of emotions and circumstances. Further, I am immeasurably grateful that my country never called upon me to make the ultimate sacrifice of giving up my own life. Many Americans were not so fortunate. Regardless of your world views, I hope that you will always respect and honor the memories of those who made the ultimate sacrifice for our country.

As a nation, we collectively honor these brave souls on Memorial Day. Memorial Day is a day of joy—parades and barbecues with family and friends. We celebrate those who made the ultimate sacrifice in defense of our great nation, our way of life, and our freedom. But, there was a time in my life when Memorial Day made me uncomfortable. Celebrating death felt odd to me. I see things differently now.

At the time that I write this, approximately 1.1 million Americans have died fighting in uniform. Our minds have difficulty grasping the reality of such a number. You would agree that 1.1 million deaths are horrible, but can you comprehend that behind each one of those deaths was an individual with hopes, dreams, family, and friends? You've had (or will have) a loved one pass away. The pain, confusion, and grief caused by these losses are beyond description. Of the 1.1 million sacrifices we honor, let's grab just one person out of that statistic. Assume the actual number is 1,100,001 and we are going to grab that stray "1" and think about him for a moment.

We'll call him Tony. Tony was a star high school football player in Des Moines, Iowa and an excellent guitarist, thanks to his grandfather's tutelage. He enlisted in the Marines after high school to serve his country because Tony believed in America and believed in the American spirit—he was also tough as nails. After his first tour of duty, Tony married his high school sweetheart, Juliette. Juliette was a middle school history teacher and a gifted painter. Their twin boys, Michael and Joseph, were preschoolers whose days were filled with reckless abandon. Getting them to sit quietly through church each week required divine intervention.

One day, Tony had to leave home for deployment. He and Juliette cried softly as they said goodbye. Michael and Joseph hugged their father goodbye, and both were adamant in their only request—"Go get the bad guys, Daddy!"

Months later, Tony's platoon was ambushed. Tony never had a chance. His wounds were fatal, but his death was not immediate. He screamed and writhed in unspeakable pain as the black blood pooled out of his wounds. Surviving members of his platoon held his hand tightly as Tony bled out. His screams of pain softened into boyish cries for his mother, his wife, and his children . . . and then to a whisper as he prayed to God as his mouth gushed blood. There was no hospital bed, friendly nurse attendant, or family gathering in his final moments on Earth. He was thousands of miles away from his home, afraid, and alone, except for his brothers-in-arms who wept as they dutifully and delicately placed his corpse in a body bag.

War is hell. I didn't enjoy writing that, and I know you didn't enjoy reading it. If you were to read the equivalent story of each unique sacrifice among the 1.1 million fallen military we honor, you would need years without sleep to do so. We cannot possibly attempt to process the details of 1.1 million deaths, but we can accept and reflect on the horror that they endured. "Tony" had hopes, dreams and a vision for his future. On the day of his death, he had no warning that those dreams were placed squarely in the crosshairs of the enemy's weapon.

If Tony, from the other side, watched your Memorial Day, how would he want you to celebrate? How would he want you to live? The answers to these questions explain my change of heart about Memorial Day. I don't know Tony because he's a fictional character, representative of the sacrificed men and women we honor, but I have a pretty good idea of what his answers would be. He would ask us to celebrate with joy and love. He would ask us to cherish every moment with our loved ones—along with each bite of our hot dogs and sip of our beers.

What is our obligation to Tony beyond a Memorial Day celebration? When he enlisted in the Marine Corps, he handed a check to our country. The check was written in the amount of "all I have, up to and including my life." Tony didn't die in excruciating pain in a foreign land because he wanted to. He died defending our nation and our way of life. I suspect if you asked Tony what our obligation is to him, he would respond as Tom Hanks' character in the movie *Saving Private Ryan* did—"Earn it." You "earn it" by living freely where you stand. You don't have to take up arms and fight our enemies overseas. Still, you have to embrace the responsibility of doing whatever you can, whenever you can, wherever you are, to carry on the American traditions for which Tony selflessly sacrificed himself. What traditions? The traditions of chasing your destiny, helping your neighbors, leading your community, and raising your family with values of honor, respect, and virtue.

Tony died defending America in a foreign land, but there is always work to do on the great American experiment right here on our soil. We are the defenders of freedom and liberty on the domestic front. How do you defend this front? Lead! Lead your family, neighborhood, community, church, city, county, state, and nation by helping, mentoring, and honoring each other. We need local leaders who recognize that we, the people, with our God-given rights, hold the American spirit in our hearts. This spirit, which knows no surrender, perseveres through all and is the bedrock of our freedom and liberty.

After writing this letter, I considered deleting it. Do you need such a morbid message about our fallen soldiers? As you know, because you are reading this, I changed my mind. I think it is necessary for you to have an appreciation of the cost of war. The older I get, the less I understand the necessity of war. However, upon reflection, I always come back to the same conclusion—there is evil in the world. There are people in this world who want to do us harm. I wish this weren't true, but history has shown us that it is. Combatting this evil is necessary. The brave men and women who gave up their lives in that combat should always hold a special place in your heart.

*Love,*
*Dad*

*Dear Hunter*

NFL teams score approximately 30 percent more points in the 4th quarter than they do in the 1st quarter. If you're a football fan, this shouldn't surprise you. The success of the "two-minute drill" is astounding. With only 60 minutes to play, I would think a team would treat each second of the first two minutes of a game as sacredly as the last two. Of course, there are physical stamina issues in an NFL game to consider, but in our lives, very few of us have physical stamina issues to consider in regard to achieving our dreams in the time we are given.

Why do so many people live life like it's the first quarter instead of the fourth quarter? *I'll get to that later. Tomorrow, I'll tackle that. Maybe next year, I'll pursue my dreams. I'm not ready for that yet.* Sound familiar? Where's our sense of urgency? If not now, when? Living with "4th quarter" passion has nothing to do with age. Your time on earth is limited; there is no guarantee of tomorrow. Today is the only day when anything can be achieved.

So, what stops us from living with a sense of urgency? Why are so many of us prone to bouts of procrastination? I hope, for your sake, that procrastination is not genetic because both your mother and I are chronic procrastinators. I've struggled with procrastination my entire life, and I have found it to be debilitating at times. I've thought through this tendency often and have come to believe that procrastination can usually be traced back to feelings of fear and inadequacy. "Perfectionism" is often the named culprit, but this is just a fancy way to dress up fear. Our fear is that if we can't do something perfectly, we prefer not to do it at all, or least not today. Of course, this is a self-sabotaging thought because we are imperfect people, and everything we do is imperfect. Where this gets tricky is separating what we know intellectually from what we feel emotionally. I can "know" that procrastinating is not a winning strategy for me but overcoming the emotions that underpin this tendency is easier said than done.

- Here are a few ways to assist you in transitioning from 1st quarter living to 4th quarter living and overcoming procrastination.

- Gratitude. Spend at least five minutes a day reviewing the things in your life for which you are thankful. Be sure to include "time." Be grateful for the time you have been given and for the time you have in front of you. I have heard that gratitude is the key to happiness, and to be honest, for years I never really accepted this. However, as I age, I realize that the benefit of reflecting on your gratitude is the powerful mindset that you create when you do so. Specifically, as you practice gratitude, your mindset will shift to one that believes that the universe is in your corner, versus pitted against you. With this new-found mindset, you are more inclined to tackle the tasks that stand between you and your dreams.

- Don't count sheep at night. Instead, repeat the word "now" 50—yes--50 times before you go to sleep at night. In the morning, repeat the word "now" during your morning routine. Play with the word: *Now. Now! Now? Now?!* Just keep repeating it. I recommend this exercise if, and only if, you are struggling with procrastination. Living with a sense of urgency is a skill that needs to be cultivated and balanced. Living with a sense of undue urgency is a recipe for anxiety. This exercise will program your mind in a way that I have found to be very powerful, especially when my mind is planning to work "tomorrow, tomorrow, tomorrow."

- Sometimes "good" is good enough. Perfectionists routinely over-estimate the time a particular task will take because they have a bias towards completing the task perfectly. The thought process behind that tendency is admirable. Who could argue with attacking every task with the intent of performing to their maximum capability? This philosophy sounds like a winning strategy, but the reality is much different. In every project or task you tackle, there is a point of diminishing return. More specifically, you will get to a point in a project where the additional resources you dedicate are not worth the results they return. Perfect is the enemy of done. Take this letter as an example. There is no doubt in my mind that I could spend the next two years refining my thoughts for you. However, what's better? A letter that is good and done, or a letter that is on its way to perfect but never completed?

- Move the needle. Assume your progress towards achieving your dreams is being monitored on a gauge. Are your actions moving the needle forward in a meaningful way? Sometimes, we fool ourselves into thinking we are taking action towards achieving our dreams by staying busy, but "busy" isn't synonymous with "productive." Need a litmus test? Imagine you had only one month to achieve your dream, what would you be working on and what would you let go? In most endeavors, 20 percent of your efforts result in 80 percent of the results. Identify what constitutes the impactful 20 percent and focus on that work.

- Measure. Quantify an element that is central to your success and then measure it, every single day. Further, place your measurement in a location that is highly visible to you. The power of visually seeing the progress, or lack of progress, towards your goal cannot be understated. If you think you have a dream that you would like to achieve that cannot be quantified, think harder.

- Peer Pressure. Many people do not share their dreams because they fear that if they don't achieve them, they will appear foolish to those that know about the dream. Let this fear go. This is the fourth quarter; you need all the help that you can get. Let the world know what you intend to achieve, or at least let a few close friends know. There is unspeakable power in this single act. You will find yourself shifting into 4th quarter living when your reputation is on the line. It is amazing how the universe will move mountains for you when you make your intentions known. In the spirit of practicing what you preach, I will share with you that my dream is to become a *New York Times* bestselling author. There, I said it. You can too.

Flip the script on your fears. Between you and your dream is a substantial amount of fear around which there is no path. You will have to go through this fear head on—fear of the unknown, fear of failure, fear of rejection, etc. There are no loopholes. Be courageous. As John Wayne said, "Courage is being scared to death, but saddling up anyway." To make matters worse, each day that passes where you ignore or avoid these fears causes them to grow stronger. These fears have been haunting you for so long. Isn't it exhausting?

- Never wait for motivation. Motivation is a thief—a thief of time and opportunity. He promises to call soon. He promises to spend more time with you. He is a liar. Motivation arrives through one path, and one path only—action. Action creates motivation. The grand illusion of life is that motivation creates action. In the 1st quarter, we can believe this fallacy, but in the 4th quarter, it's time to admit that motivation is a lark. Action creates motivation. Therefore, no matter how beat down you may feel, if you want motivation to join you in your travels, you must act first. Action—now, now, now.

*Love,*

*Dad*

*Dear Hunter*

In 2003, I had just completed a three-year assignment on a fast-attack nuclear submarine out of Norfolk, Virginia. It was time for me to rotate to a shore duty assignment. These assignments are typically land-based duties such as instructors, schedulers, or inspectors; however, I volunteered for duty in the Middle East in support of Operation Iraqi Freedom. Why? Good question. At the time, I was motivated by a desire to contribute to the War on Terrorism in a manner that was more face-to-face than submarine service allows. Why? Good question. I felt that I had something to prove to myself. I wanted to prove that I wasn't afraid to come face-to-face with evil and fight back. During this assignment, I learned a lot about myself and about courage. Although, as is true with many life lessons, what I learned surprised me.

I recall a time in the Arabian Gulf when I was assigned to lead a team that was tasked with boarding vessels to search for contraband leaving—and terrorists fleeing—Iraq. I had no experience to speak of in doing such operations; however, like many assignments in the military, you learn as you go. I was assigned to a Coast Guard water patrol boat, USCGC Adak (WPB-1333). I met the U.S. military team that I would be leading for a brief discussion about recent intelligence and mission objectives. As I was briefing the mission, I could see that the members of this team were looking at me suspiciously. Although I was wearing the desert combat uniform just like they were, the submarine warfare insignia on my badge created some confusion. I could hear their unspoken words. Why is there a submarine officer directing a boarding operation in the Northern Arabian Gulf? This team had conducted hundreds of boarding operations. I had conducted zero. However, I recall someone saying that courage is being the only one who knows just how terrified you are. Although I did my best to make sure this was true, I doubt I was successful. This was the first assignment of my military career where I would be face-to-face with danger in a very real sense. I think the team sensed this.

We launched the seven-person RHIB (rigid hull inflated boat) from the Adak. As we approached our first target, an Iraqi fishing vessel, I felt my blood surge as my mind flooded with endorphins. We pulled alongside the vessel, but as they had no intentions of letting us board their vessel, they began evasive maneuvers. Each time we matched their course and speed and narrowed the distance between the two vessels, they evaded. The pounding of the waves against our small RHIB was doing a number on my stomach. In the blink of an eye, the distance between the two ships narrowed and steadied to allow members of our team to begin boarding this vessel. I was the last one to do so. Perhaps it goes without saying, but in case not, there was no welcome ladder to utilize. The process of boarding the vessel made me feel like a pirate. I literally threw myself out of the RHIB and grabbed the vessel's side and then scaled my way onto the deck. It may have only been a few feet away and six feet high, but it felt like hundreds. As I was scaling the side of this fishing vessel, not knowing what awaited us on deck, I remember asking myself, *What decisions did I make in life that have led me to this place? I am a nuclear engineer and a submarine officer. Now I am throwing myself aboard fishing vessels in the Northern Arabian Gulf searching for AK-47 rifles and terrorists.*

I did, in time, grow more comfortable with the process of boarding vessels in the Arabian Gulf. I am not sharing this story because I believe I was being courageous. I do not believe that. However, I realized something about courage from the process. I realized that courage is not the absence of fear. Courage is feeling fear and then doing what must be done anyway. I think there are many people who fail to live courageously because they expect the fear to go away. I was lucky because I was forced to face my fear and do my job. There were no options available to me. In life, this is usually not the case. In fact, I would go so far as to say that like in my case, when you have no options but to face your fears, that isn't real courage. Real courage is when you face your fears even though you have the option of running away. This is especially challenging when doing the right thing in the face of your fears is not supported by those around you. I would describe this as mental courage, which can really test a person's mettle.

I recall a time on a submarine mission when I failed to demonstrate mental courage, and it haunts me to this day. Nuclear submarines have arsenals of weapons that should strike fear into the hearts of our enemies. One of these weapons is the Tomahawk missile—a long-range and highly precise weapon used to attack land-based targets. The perfect execution of firing these advanced missiles is the most critical element to a successful Tomahawk strike. There are several complex variables that must be managed on a nuclear submarine during a Tomahawk strike mission. Therefore, submarine crews spend a lot of time training on this mission through simulated attack scenarios. These training scenarios are conducted with an intensity that can exceed an actual strike. If a nuclear submarine crew can excel during the simulated strikes, the actual mission typically appears simple by comparison. The reason for this is that those training scenarios include preparing for everything that can go wrong: a change in mission at the last second, equipment faults that impact the ship's ability to fire the missiles, and weapon malfunctions that are possible, but highly unlikely. Create a training scenario with one or more of these contingencies and the scenario becomes intense.

The intensity of the exercise is challenging to describe. There are no discernible clues to remind any of the people in control that this is just an exercise. The ship is at sea, submerged at periscope depth in an environment designed to simulate war-like conditions to the maximum extent. The command-and-control unit ashore is communicating directions, orders, and changes with the same tone and tempo as it would in an actual attack. The only difference is that the weapons do not leave the ship.

To support these training scenarios, nuclear submarines will sometimes bring a simulator, called a TOTEM (Tomahawk test missile) out to sea with them. The TOTEM is the same size as an actual Tomahawk missile (20+ feet long and 21 inches in diameter). A TOTEM increases the effectiveness of the training because it communicates directly with the submarine's Fire Control system. This allows the TOTEM to simulate malfunctions that provide the operators with identical indications that would occur in an actual casualty.

Fast forward to a strike exercise that occurred aboard a nuclear submarine using a TOTEM as a training device. For context, I was the Communications Officer and was standing directly next to the Combat System Officer (WEPS).

"In the open window, salvo one. Fire when ready," the Commanding Officer bellowed.

"Fire when ready, aye sir," reported the WEPS.

A "salvo" implies a series of launches in rapid succession. Therefore, the WEPS began to direct a series of orders to launch missiles at exactly the correct time (within seconds). In response to these orders, the operators have to simulate most switch manipulations to prevent an actual launch of a missile. However, whenever practicable, our training program allows operators to physically manipulate switches to maximize the training value. One way to do this during strike exercises is to physically launch "waterslugs" out of empty torpedo tubes. If a torpedo tube is empty, the tube can be flooded with seawater and equalized with sea pressure, and then the high-pressure air system that would normally impulse the launch of a torpedo or a Tomahawk missile is applied to a slug of water. If the tube is empty, the operators can proceed with an actual launch, resulting in a slug of water leaving the ship at a high velocity. It sounds really cool and adds to the realistic training.

After simulating a few missile launches from salvo one, the WEPS ordered the Weapon's Control Console (WCC) operator, "In the open window, shoot tube two."

The WCC operator, a 10-year veteran with an impeccable professional reputation among the crew and officers responded, "Shoot tube two, aye" and began to simulate the launch of tube two.

The WEPS abruptly stopped him. "Tube two is empty" (code for we can shoot a waterslug) and continued, "Shoot tube two."

I recall thinking, *There's a TOTEM loaded in tube two!*

The WCC calmly responded, "Sir, there is a TOTEM loaded in tube two. Simulating the launch of tube two."

I was relieved to hear the WCC say this. Launching a TOTEM into the ocean would make for a bad day for us all.

The WEPS was an aggressive and intense leader.

The WEPS didn't skip a beat in response to this report. "Tube two is empty. SHOOT tube two."

The WCC operator held his ground. "No sir. There is a TOTEM loaded in tube two."

*C'mon on WEPS! Back off. He's right*, I thought.

For further context, I was a junior officer aboard this submarine but had been on the submarine long enough to feel pretty comfortable in my assignments. However, the WEPS was a senior officer, and I was not accustomed to standing up to or disagreeing with senior officers. Although I had been trained to do "the right thing" even when it was uncomfortable, I had not adequately prepared for this moment. I had the opportunity to stop a bad situation from getting worse, but I didn't. Instead, I did nothing.

You may be able to predict where this story is headed. Instinctually, so did everyone else in the control room. The intensity and volume of the dialogue between the WEPS and the WCC operator began to draw people's attention. For a strike exercise, the control room is jam-packed and includes nearly every officer aboard. The following people were within 10 feet of the WEPS: the Commanding Officer, the Executive Officer, the Engineer Officer, the Navigation/ Operations Officer, and the Communications Officer—me. In addition, there were at least 20 enlisted personnel in the control room. All of the other people in the control room had their own assignments that required their full attention. However, everyone's "spidey" sense had been lit up—this was only an exercise; if there is a dispute about the status of tube two, why not pause the training to clarify what, if anything, was loaded into tube two?

However, the window for someone to provide this type of backup was of a small duration and quickly closing.

The WEPS bellowed into the ear of the WCC, "Tube two is empty, shoot tube two. That is an order."

*Say something, Matt. Stop this!* I thought. But I couldn't find the courage to do anything.

The WCC fought valiantly to protect against the upcoming untoward event, but without the support of anyone else in the control room and his obligation to obey direct and legal orders, his options quickly dissipated. The tone of his voice was a combination of resignation and "I told you so" when he eventually relinquished, "Shoot tube two, Aye Sir."

Moments later the multimillion-dollar training simulator was launched into the Atlantic Ocean in search of its final resting place at the bottom of the ocean several thousand feet below. No one was hurt. Life went on. But accidentally launching something from a nuclear submarine is not a good day in the life of a submariner.

Why didn't I do something? Why didn't I say, *Stop! Training timeout. I recommend we verify the status of tube two prior to proceeding*? If I had, the humiliating, expensive, and potentially dangerous mistake would have certainly been averted. I've thought long and hard about the answers to those questions over the years. There are many reasons why I didn't act, but the root cause to my inaction was inadequate preparation. Courage, especially mental courage, requires one to pre-train the brain to prepare for situations such as these. Have you asked yourself questions about how you would handle various situations? For example: you observe your boss behaving unethically, you observe a coworker harassing another coworker, or you witness a senior officer acting recklessly. What will you do? Find out in advance. Work through the scenario and determine your course of action. Be prepared.

These mental exercises do not prepare you for an "if" scenario, they prepare you for a "when" scenario. Life WILL test your mental courage, and often you won't have the time to consider all of the available options. Your mind will default to inaction if you haven't previously prepared yourself. Of course, you can't prepare yourself for every possible scenario, but you can bias your mind towards taking action when doing the "right thing" might otherwise be challenging.

*Love,*
*Dad*

*Dear Hunter*

Baseball has been a part of my life since as far back as I can remember. I think it is fair to say that baseball was my first true love. I vividly remember the excitement of going to Tony's Stationary store with a dollar and coming out with four packs of 1980 Topps baseball cards. I remember the unbridled enthusiasm of being seven years old and attending my first practice with the midget league team, the Lion's Club. I remember the thrill of winning the championship with the Lion's Club that same year. My life events are earmarked with baseball milestones—my first game pitching in 3rd grade, my first stolen base in 4th grade, my first losing season in 5th grade with Paul's Motors little league team, and my first little league all-star game in 6th grade. The list goes on.

I always dreamed of becoming a major league baseball player, and I don't recall exactly when that dream died, but I do recall how my baseball career ended. The year was 1992 and I was a senior in high school. Graduation was only a few short weeks away, and a few short months after that I'd be attending Rutgers University. Despite all of the typical distractions that come with being a senior in high school in May, there was one activity that my friends and I remained laser-focused on—baseball. The group of friends that comprised our high school varsity baseball team had been playing together since 2nd grade. We were regional all-star team champions in elementary school, and, as we grew up, the expectations for us grew as well. We didn't disappoint in our senior year of high school. We finished the regular season with a 27-1 record and were among the top-ranked high school teams in the state. To this day, I can name every player on that team and remain friends with most of them. Going into the state championship game, tensions and expectations were high. We had a flame throwing junior, Tommy, pitching that day, and we were confident in our chances to walk off the field as state champions. The game seemed to fly by with neither team producing much offense. In the blink of an eye, it was the last inning—and we were losing 2-1. We were three outs away from the end of our high school baseball careers, and what we did with those three outs would determine if we would end our childhood baseball journey as state champions or not.

I do not remember the specifics of the first two outs of that final inning. What I do remember is coming to the plate with two outs and the tying run on 2nd base. I remember glancing over into the stands and seeing the cheering faces of our classmates, teachers, and families. It was a familiar scene filled with faces that had cheered us on since 2nd grade. *Wow. This is how it's going to be, huh? Two outs, bottom of the ninth, tying run on 2nd base for the state championship, in front of all of your family and friends . . . and you're at the plate. Let's do this, Matt!* I felt as relaxed and confident as I could be, considering the circumstances.

The first pitch was a fastball right down the middle of the plate. Strike one. No big deal as I wasn't planning on swinging at the first pitch. The next pitch was a fastball, low and outside. Ball one. Then came a curve ball which I put a good swing on but fouled off. *Deep breath. Two strikes.* The final pitch was a high fastball, likely a ball, but I swung . . . and missed. Strike three. I felt the weight of my entire team's baseball hopes and dreams crushing my chest. I was stunned. I just struck out to lose the state championship game. How could this have happened? This wasn't the script! We were the team destined to win. I was supposed to be the hero. In the blink of an eye, all of my baseball memories would forever be viewed through the lens of this sinking feeling. I don't remember what I did, or what I said, or even the bus ride home, but I never forgot that moment, and I never will.

I could tell you that "time heals all wounds" and that I learned to put a high school baseball game into perspective as the years passed. I could, but I would be lying. There is probably not a day that goes by that I don't think about that at-bat.

So now what? What can I say to you? Don't strike out to lose the state championship baseball game? The heartbreak that I experienced in the batter's box that day was deep. As I mentioned, baseball was my first love and as Rod Stewart says, "The first cut is the deepest." I have certainly had my fair share of disappointments before and since that day, and I do have advice for you on how to avoid feeling the sting of disappointment in your life. It is surefire advice that I guarantee will protect you from ever feeling let down. The approach is simple: Do nothing. Say nothing. Go nowhere. If you follow these three simple rules, I assure you that you will escape the stinging tail of the disappointment whip.

If you choose to ignore this approach, the second piece of advice I have for you is to develop a short memory. Admittedly, I think the lack of a short memory limited me in my athletic endeavors. I have developed a shorter memory in my professional career, but I'm still working on developing this. Most of the world's successful athletes, businesspeople, inventors, and leaders have this in common—they have a very short memory. They know how to let disappointments and failures go and move on to the next challenge, the next game, or next at-bat. Michael Jordan has a famous quote about failure that resonates with me: "I've missed more than 9,000 shots in my career. I've lost almost 300 games. Twenty-six times I've been trusted to take the game-winning shot and missed. I've failed over and over and over again in my life. And that is why I succeed."

What I've come to realize is that failure and disappointment are both part of a life well-lived. When you reflect on a failure or disappointment, please know that although there is nothing that can take away the sting; the absence of failures and disappointments likely means you are living life too safely. I hope that you will live a life that is full of going-for-the-gold and swinging-for-the fences moments because doing so helps keep your eyes on opportunity and possibility. There are plenty of people who live life trying to avoid the strikeout or the disappointment, and in doing so, shun life's beauty and promise. View your failures as battle scars of a life lived well. As much as that scar of striking out still causes me pain, I wouldn't trade it away because it means that I loved something fiercely and loving fiercely is living life fully.

Another element of failure worth exploring is fear of failure. Dealing with failure is one thing, you can live with that. Failing to embrace life's opportunities because you are afraid of failure is not something you can live with. Doing so may save you some scars, but the cumulative weight of opportunity lost is something you will carry in your soul, which will eventually become too heavy to bear. If your car is in a tailspin and you want to avoid hitting the tree on the side of the road, the best guidance is to focus your eyes on where you want the car to go, not on the tree you don't want to hit. The thought process behind this guidance is that your mind will seek out what you think about. If you think about striking out, even if you are thinking, "Don't strike out. Don't strike out. Don't strike out.", you are more likely to strike out. Train your brain to focus on what you want, not on what you want to avoid. The universe and your mind have an uncanny ability to conspire with or against you in the form of materializing your thoughts. Feed your brain with optimism and possibility, not doubt and fear.

*Love,*
*Dad*

*Dear Hunter*

When I was in sixth grade, there was a girl in my class whom the other students picked on. I had known her since the first grade, and although we weren't "friends," we were always friendly to each other. There were a couple of kids in the class who started to get more aggressive in their treatment of her. I recall a day when one of the students brought in a bag of dog treats and placed them on her desk. The class cracked up, and many students started to bark like dogs. I will never forget the look on the girl's face as she stared at the bag of dog treats on her desk while her classmates barked at her. I saw a tear run down her cheek. She hung her head and accepted the situation passively. She said and did nothing. Do you know who else said and did nothing? Me. That moment is one of my biggest life regrets. The image of her face as the class taunted, barked and laughed at her is seared into my memory, and the regret of my inaction weighs heavily on my soul.

Sadly, and much to my chagrin, this was not an isolated incident. Throughout my childhood, I watched other students get picked on and bullied. The aggressiveness and violence of this treatment got worse as we got older. In high school, there was a boy on my basketball team who was routinely beaten up in the locker room before and after practice. I watched a group of boys hit him, kick him, spit on him, and rip his clothes—not just once or twice but almost every day. He was a nice kid. I had known him all my life. Why was he treated this way? More importantly, why did I not do anything? Although I didn't participate in the beatings, turning a blind eye was, in some ways, worse. I was complicit in this horrible treatment. I was the team captain. Let me say that again: I was the team captain. To this day, I view my inaction and silence as the biggest leadership failure of my lifetime.

Truth be told, I would prefer not to share these stories with you because I am ashamed of them. However, if I don't, I fear that you will make the same mistakes that I did. I was raised in a household that valued respect, compassion, and empathy. These are the same values that your mother and I have tried to model for you. These values create a foundation for living that I am hopeful you will build upon in your lifetime. Clearly, seeing my parents model these values was not enough to drive me into action when I observed these values breached outside of the home. I think I was under the impression that the rules at school were different than the rules at home. I witnessed teachers turning a blind eye to bullying. I think I justified my inaction by assuming that some people were just meant to be bullied. Honestly, I was just thankful that I wasn't one of them. I am cringing as I write these words. They were horrible events and actions, but they are the truth.

As I got older, I watched bullying become less violent but harmful, nonetheless. Adults are less apt to kick, push, and punch, but that doesn't mean that adults stop preying on the weak. On my first submarine assignment, there was an officer who struggled to fit in. He was routinely delinquent on his qualification process. His leadership skills were lacking. He seemed to be the butt of every joke in the wardroom. Once again, I did nothing to help him. I was the most junior officer on the submarine at the time, and I was simply thankful that no one was picking on me.

It is sad to think about, but there is truth to the fact that people tend to pick on the weak. We have an innate desire to climb the social ladder. Often, this desire manifests itself as pushing others down in a subconscious effort to raise our own status. Further, instead of shunning bullies, the harsh reality is that bullies are often very popular. Again, this is a result of an evolutionary desire to be at the top of the pack's social status. I would encourage you to recognize this tendency and fight through it. There is no social ladder worth climbing if it requires you to participate, directly or indirectly, in terrorizing and humiliating those who are weaker than you.

As a form of penance for my own shortcomings, I want to make something very clear to you. You cannot turn a blind eye to bullying. It is not an option for the life of virtue and values that I hope for you. There is nothing more noble and virtuous than standing up for people who need help. The best time to cultivate this habit is in kindergarten; the second-best time is today. Make no mistake, what I am asking you to do requires uncommon courage. However, failing to exhibit that courage by standing up for others will result in a very heavy weight of regret, which I know all about because I carry that weight. The irony of this social ladder metaphor is that when you do stand up for those who are being bullied, your status among your peers will skyrocket. Very few people are comfortable with bullying, but fewer people have the courage to do anything about it. Make yourself an exception to that rule and watch how, in time, the right people gravitate towards you. Those who don't recognize your courage are likely toxic people, and you're better off without them in your life.

To further help you understand the challenges of sticking up for someone who is being bullied, you should understand the psychological theory called the bystander effect. The bystander effect is a widely accepted belief that the more people witnessing a victim in need, the less likely anyone is to help. As an example, imagine you are walking down a busy street in New York City. The sidewalk is a virtual sea of people. On the curb there is an old man crying out in pain. Because the street is so crowded, the likelihood that you will render assistance is less than it would be if the streets were deserted. The bystander effect asserts that the more people available to help, the more likely we are to assume that someone else will help. Plant a seed in your mind now that your willingness to help others must be a function of the need that you are witnessing, not the size of the crowd that is available to help. The words of Albert Einstein ring true to me: "The world is a dangerous place to live; not because of the people who are evil, but because of the people who don't do anything about it."

Of course, there is a flip side to this discussion. What if you are the one that is being bullied? My heart aches to even consider this possibility for you, but it is likely that you will be on the receiving end of some form of bullying at some point in your life. Most bullies are the same—they have learned to inflate and feed their egos by pushing other people down. Additionally, most bullies are lazy. The world is full of people to bully, and most people will cave to the aggressive behavior of those who choose to prey on the weak. If you can walk away, walk away. If you have a quick wit, attempt to disarm the bully with humor. I do not condone violence as a problem-solving measure; however, if you have no options, defend yourself—violently. Above all, keep showing up. The worst thing that you can do is give up on your hopes and dreams because of a bully. I think back to the boy on my high school basketball team that I mentioned earlier in this letter. His name is Eric. Eric was a sports fanatic but, truth be told, was not a very good athlete. In fact, he rarely got to play in games but always showed up to practices. I didn't appreciate his courage and determination then, but I do now. Regardless of the bullying he was subjected to, Eric showed up to practice every day—day after day, month after month, and year after year. There was no stopping Eric, and I admire him immensely for having that kind of courage. I don't know what has become of Eric, but I can assure you that wherever he is and whatever he is doing, he is a mentally tough character worthy of admiration.

*Love,*
*Dad*

*Dear Hunter*

During my MBA program at the University of Connecticut, I took a course called Organizational Management. Dr. Palmer was the professor, and he routinely had the class conduct exercises that revealed elements of human behavior. These exercises were always very enlightening, but there was one that has stuck with me that I'd like to share with you.

Dr. Palmer set the stage for the exercise by giving us information about non-verbal communication. This would prove to be a red herring. However, he dutifully presented 30 minutes of material about the basics of non-verbal communication, including how prevalent non-verbal communication was in the workplace. In fact, I recall him stating that 75 percent of information is transmitted in the workplace via non-verbal cues. He then had us break into groups of six with each group at its own table. He explained that we would be playing a new card game—the catch was that once the game started, there would be no verbal communication allowed. We would have to play the game and keep score using only non-verbal communication. He passed out a copy of the rules of the game to each table. We had 10 minutes to read the rules and discuss how we would play and keep score, but after those 10 minutes, no talking would be allowed. Further, he informed us that after 10 minutes of play, the person with the highest score would move to another group.

Keep in mind that we were a group of hard-charging, motivated, MBA students, so we took this exercise very seriously. I recall my group having a great strategy for conducting play and keeping score with only non-verbal communication. When play began we executed our strategy flawlessly. Dr. Palmer informed us when 10 minutes had passed. The winner moved to another table, and our group had a new player from another group. This is when the exercise got interesting.

As we started the second round, our strategy was less than flawless. The new player was a monkey wrench in our finely tuned non-verbal machine. Not only was it challenging to get the scoring correct because he wasn't part of the group when we verbally agreed on how we would score the game; it seemed as if he didn't understand the game that he was playing. For example, if aces were a high card and sevens were wild, he seemed to think that aces were low, and threes were wild. Because we weren't allowed to talk, his confusion created frustration amongst this ultra-competitive group of MBA students. The challenges with this new player continued. We rolled our eyes in frustration. How could he be so stupid? The rules weren't that difficult. In time, he seemed to get on board or at least acquiesce to the group.

A new round started, and we experienced a similar challenge. The new player at the table didn't grasp the rules. Again, the group collectively sighed with exasperation.

Soon, Dr. Palmer ended the exercise and explained to us what was happening. The purpose of the exercise had nothing to do with non-verbal communication. The purpose of the exercise was to examine how we reacted to people outside our group who were operating with different assumptions. Dr. Palmer had given each table a different set of instructions for how to play the card game. Therefore, the new person at the table wasn't wrong, they were just operating with a different set of rules. The interesting part of the exercise, and the part that has stuck with me since that day, was his question about what we thought of the new person in the group. He asked, "Did you consider that maybe there was a logical explanation for why the new people at the table didn't understand the rules? Or did you just assume that they were misinformed or stupid?" We exchanged glances of humility at our table. The truth was that we assumed the worst in the new people. We assumed that they didn't understand the rules. In fact, as we discussed our emotions candidly, we further confessed that we had thoughts like, "Is this person stupid?"

Dr. Palmer went on to explain that these reactions are normal. In fact, he expanded the discussion to the context of culture. When a person moves from one culture to another, they are often operating under a different set of rules and assumptions. These rules and assumptions are not better or worse but different. The people in the new culture, however, will not instinctually make allowances for this. Quite the contrary, the people in the new culture will often think the worst of the person. They will assume that they are stupid, or slow, or somehow "less than." This rang true to me. I thought back to times in my life when I encountered a person from a different country, or even a different state, and I reflected upon how I thought of that person when they had different expectations about social interactions.

Additionally, these reflections led me to learn about a cognitive bias called the actor-observer bias, or the fundamental attribution error. This cognitive bias causes us to attribute external factors to problems that we have, but internal factors to problems that others have. For example, in the card game, if I were the one that changed tables I would be more likely to assume that something was wrong with this new group's interpretation of the rules than I would be to assume I was making a mistake. Conversely, as discussed, if someone new to the group didn't know the rules, we are more apt to blame them than search for an explanation that relieves them of any wrongdoing. Since learning the fundamental attribution error, I have learned to be more honest with myself (not all my problems can be blamed on external factors) and more open-minded when interacting with others.

My reflection brought me back to a time when I was serving in the Middle East. I was assigned as the officer in charge of planning an international naval exercise. The exercise was a five-day event with navies from 15 different countries represented. The preparations for the exercise began several months prior to the exercise itself. I recall the initial planning conference that was held in Manama, Bahrain with representatives from each of the 15 countries. I was the chair of the meeting, and I was all business. I was so focused on executing the agenda that I failed to consider whether each country had the same rules and assumptions about the exercise. For some, the exercise was a social event, for others it was an obligation, for others it was an opportunity to learn, for others it was an opportunity to show off their military prowess. All of this is clear to me in retrospect, but I was oblivious to it at the time. I approached my task the same way as I would have approached the task if everyone there was from my hometown of Hawthorne, NJ. The exercise was a success as measured by United States Navy standards. It was executed smartly, on time, and with no injuries. However, I can't help but wonder how I would have approached the assignment differently had I been equipped with the take-aways from Dr. Palmer's exercise.

I encourage you to always look for opportunities to reflect upon what different rules and assumptions others may be applying towards any given situation. I think you will find that whether someone is from a different part of the globe, a different state, or even a different family, it is likely that they are approaching the situation from a different perspective than you are. Ignore this fact at your own risk. There is rarely, if ever, one reality in life. It is tempting to assume that your reality is THE reality, but a much more accurate representation is to consider that your reality is only one among many realities. You will be well served by striving to understand other people's truths. Seek to understand before seeking to be understood.

*Love,*
*Dad*

*Dear Hunter*

I was living in Kansas City, Missouri when I started going to a boxing gym. I was getting into great physical and mental shape and was really enjoying this method of physical fitness. During my time there, I became friendly with one of the trainers Josh. I started personal training sessions with Josh to augment the group classes that I was attending. Josh was in his mid-20s, a mixed-martial arts fighter, and a very friendly and engaging individual. We had a few one-on-one sessions together, and I really enjoyed training with him. For the most part we focused on boxing, but we were slowly getting to know a little bit about each other on a personal level.

Josh called me at 10 p.m. one night from jail. He was arrested on an outstanding warrant for unpaid fines related to a DUI arrest. I could hear the embarrassment in his voice when he confessed that he had no one else to call. Josh told me that he had to pay $2,000 in fines in order to be released from jail. He said that he completely understood if I couldn't help, but again, he had no one else to call. My initial instinct was to politely tell him that unfortunately, I couldn't be of help, because after all, I barely knew Josh. But a thought washed over me and convinced me otherwise. The thought was a simple one: *If you can help, you should.* Don't get me wrong, $2,000 is a lot of money, but the truth was that I could help and decided that I would. I drove down to the police station, paid his fines and drove him back to his apartment. On the drive to his apartment, he confessed that he had other outstanding fines in other cities in the area and was worried that this could happen again. I recommended that we meet up later in the week for coffee so we could talk about his situation and brainstorm options.

When we met for coffee to discuss his situation, he shared a lot with me. Josh had not had an easy path in life. He was in and out of foster homes as a child. He had barely graduated high school. He used to run with a bad crowd and got himself into trouble with the law. He had unpaid federal taxes. He had multiple warrants out for his arrest. He acknowledged and owned his mistakes of the past but felt helpless to create a clean slate upon which to build a better future. As he spoke, I reflected on my background. I had been blessed with a supportive family and a path that was much more forgiving than the path Josh had travelled. For one reason or another, I committed to helping Josh clean his slate and build a better future for himself.

We put a plan together to get Josh clean with the local and federal government. This involved quite a financial investment on my part, and we agreed that he would pay me back when he could. I told him that I trusted him to do the right thing when he was in a position to do so. After a few months of cleaning the slate, our conversations, which had turned into weekly meetings at a local coffee shop, turned towards a discussion about his future. He was an aspiring MMA fighter and was making some money on the side with personal training, but he admitted that he needed to do more to keep up with his bills and set aside money for his future. We were brainstorming options for him when he mentioned that he had experience as a painter.

As soon he said this, I realized that I was faced with another major decision regarding how far I wanted to take my involvement with Josh's situation. I was the general manager of a power plant in Kansas City at the time. The plant was old and run down, and part of my efforts as the new general manager was to give the plant a face lift. I had already been discussing a plan the plant manager to paint the facility starting with the staff offices and conference rooms. We didn't have the budget to undertake a full paint job of the facility in one project, so we were going to have to find a smaller company that would be okay with doing the project a little bit at a time over the course of a few years. My vision was to get the entire five-story facility of several thousand square feet painted—the walls, the floors, the handrails, the stairs, the equipment guarding, control rooms—all of it.

The decision to pull Josh into this project wasn't simple. For starters, I worked for a several billion-dollar, multinational company. I couldn't just bring some guy into the facility and have him start painting walls. Vendors needed to be registered companies with the necessary certifications, insurances, etc. Further, there were ethical considerations at stake. As the general manager, did I really want to go down the path of having a friend of mine with no business experience compete for a large painting contract when I had no evidence of his abilities? I was in danger of crossing a line that I wasn't interested in crossing.

After much thought, I realized that I could safely test the waters by opening a project for painting only the conference room in the staff office section of the facility. I discussed the situation with the plant manager who reported to me. I told him that I had a friend who was starting a painting business and, although I could not vouch for his work, I was hopeful that we could give him a shot in painting the conference room. I asked him to treat him like he would any other contractor and ensure that all corporate requirements were met such as requiring proof of insurance, estimates, and invoices. I told the plant manager that after making the introductions I didn't want to be involved, and that he should handle all interactions with Josh since he did not have a pre-existing relationship, as I did. I also told my boss about the situation, and he was supportive of the approach that I was taking.

Of course, Josh still needed to establish, register, and insure his business even to undertake a job as small as painting the conference room. I knew how to do this, so I helped him. I explained the process to him, walked him through the steps, and within a few weeks he was the proud owner of a legitimate and fully registered painting company.

Josh proved to be tremendously professional and skilled. His paint job in the conference room and the manner in which he handled it impressed our plant manager. I asked the plant manager if he wanted to give Josh more work in the facility to which the plant manager enthusiastically responded, "Absolutely!" Josh took on more and more work at the facility and eventually had a staff of painters working around the clock tackling sections of the facility. His professionalism and his work were top-notch. I had completely removed myself from the working relationship and had the plant manager handling all the details of the painting project. The facility had never looked better, and Josh, who I continued to meet with outside of work, seemed to be in a great place—personally, professionally, and financially.

As often is the case in life, there was a "but". One of the support staff members who I had, from time to time, had a strained relationship with grew suspicious of Josh's company and my relationship with Josh. It was no secret in the plant that we knew each other. The staff member filed an ethics complaint through the company's corporate hotline. An investigation was launched, during which time I was placed on administrative leave. For more than two weeks, I sat at home twiddling my thumbs and wondering if I had overstepped a line. Although I was relatively certain that I wasn't at risk of being fired, I was less certain that my reputation in the company would survive intact. Sometimes just being accused of something makes you guilty in some people's eyes. This would be on the CEO's desk. What would he think?

The investigation cleared me of any wrongdoing, and I returned to my job. Being the center of a corporate investigation for fraud is not pleasant no matter the outcome, but I was able to move on with my life. In retrospect, did I allow my desire to help Josh cloud my professional judgment? I don't think so, but I would respect a reasonable person's conclusion that I had gotten too involved in helping Josh. This is a decision that you will have to make every time you have the opportunity to help; every time you walk by someone asking for money on the streets every time you have the opportunity to improve someone else's life. I would encourage you to stay true, without sacrificing your ability to support yourself and your family, to the *if you can help, you should* philosophy.

I'd like to end this letter with one of my favorite poems attributed to Mother Teresa entitled, "Anyway."

> *People are often unreasonable, illogical and self-centered;*
> *Forgive them anyway.*
> *If you are kind, people may accuse you of selfish, ulterior motives;*
> *Be kind anyway.*
> *If you are successful, you will win some false friends*
> *and some true enemies;*
> *Succeed anyway.*
> *If you are honest and frank, people may cheat you;*
> *Be honest and frank anyway.*
> *What you spend years building, someone could destroy overnight;*
> *Build anyway.*
> *If you find serenity and happiness, they may be jealous;*
> *Be happy anyway.*
> *The good you do today, people will often forget tomorrow;*
> *Do good anyway.*

*Give the world the best you have, and it may never be enough;*
*Give the world the best you've got anyway.*
*You see, in the final analysis, it is between you and your God;*
*It was never between you and them anyway.*

Love,
Dad

*Dear Hunter*

In 2012, I threw my hat into the ring as a candidate for the 2nd United States congressional district seat in Hawaii. Long story short, I lost the primary election. I was dejected and a bit embarrassed, but the lessons that I learned have served me well. One of the most powerful lessons that I learned was about influence. I think I previously thought that influencing people and teaching people were one and the same. *"I'm right, and here's why"* was my communication style. I was wrong, and here's why.

Unless you are discussing the solution to an algebra problem, there are no right and wrong answers in the world of social interaction. The more emotional the topic, the more this is true. Politics are a great topic to use to discuss this phenomenon because it tends to be a very emotional topic. Not only are the political topics of the day emotional for most people, but their opinions on political topics also tend to be intertwined with their perception of the world and their own self-image. Therefore, most people listen to political candidates with the intent of voting for one that sounds most aligned with their view of the world. Very few people listen to political candidates, or anyone else for that matter, to be educated. The most successful politicians are gifted at conveying their message in a way that agrees with the existing sentiment of a large cross-section of people. This runs counter to my instincts, as my more idealistic self would hope that political candidates would be self-assured, creative, and inspired enough to share their problem-solving intentions with the general public. Unfortunately, for most politicians this is not a winning strategy. In fact, most politicians do not attempt to convince anyone of anything. Instead, they attempt to find the people whose existing sentiments they can echo to get them to the polling booths on Election Day.

Even if you never throw your own hat into the political ring, there are interesting psychological phenomena at play here regarding influence and persuasion. You will find that the ability to influence and persuade other people is a powerful but fickle skill. Like I said, I used to think that "right is right" and that communicating the rationale behind "right" should be enough. As you might imagine, I didn't enjoy much success with that attitude. I made a habit of chalking up my failures to persuade by blaming the other party—*they can't handle the truth, they don't understand the truth, they are fooling themselves.* As I have matured, I have uncovered some truths that I wish were shared with me when I was younger, that I would like to share with you now.

For starters, if you want to influence others, you must learn to be an outstanding listener. Not a good listener, not a great listener, but an outstanding listener. Being an outstanding listener is not just about your ability to hear and comprehend what is being said to you; it is about conveying and communicating, without speaking, your level of interest in what is being said to you. One of my mentors in the United States Navy once told me, "No one will care how much you know, until they know how much you care." Listening intently is the most authentic and effective way to let someone know how much you care. There is no close second place. I do not believe there is a shortcut to becoming an outstanding listener. Further, I do not believe that you can become an outstanding listener through manipulation or malintent. Being an outstanding listener requires selfless and focused attention on the other person. Forget about what you plan to say next. Forget about whether you have something to say that is worth interrupting the other person for. Forget about whether the person you are listening to is right or wrong. Instead, put aside your ego and be fully present. Much like meditation is challenging if you haven't practiced, so is listening.

Next, I would encourage you to learn how to meet people where they are. I have witnessed a message falling on deaf ears because of failure to do so. When there is a gap between what you think is right and what your listener thinks is right, you will often find yourself figuratively and fruitlessly screaming across the chasm. It is far more effective to join people where they are and then lead them to a better place—one step at a time. I recall taking on a turnaround assignment in Kansas City as the plant general manager of a power plant. I was hired to fundamentally change the culture and restore the plant to financial profitability and was given a short timeline to do so. The key to success was determining where the plant leaders were, and then meeting them there. There was, in fact, a large gap between their assessment and mine, but unless I was going to tackle this project in an authoritative way—*do this, and do that, because I said so*—I knew I was going to have to join them in their current state and then lead them to a higher state. This strategy has the benefit of joining the team and then travelling together as a team. I have observed countless leaders unsuccessfully attempt to lead their teams to higher levels of performance because they failed to meet people where they were and instead attempted to communicate where they thought the team should be. Even if the leader that tries this tactic is "right", it is my observation that the success probability of this tactic is near zero.

If you are an outstanding listener and have made a habit of meeting people where they are, you are positioned to be an effective influencer.

The next habit to develop when it comes to being an effective influencer may seem counter intuitive. Specifically, don't assume you have the answers. No matter how knowledgeable you are on a subject and no matter how sure you are that you are "right"; if your objective is to influence someone else, you must drop this self-assuredness and remain open to the possibility that you don't have the answers. The more emotionally charged the subject, the more significant doing so will be. One surefire way to have someone close themselves off to your words is to reveal your motive of persuasion. If you are trying to convince your friend that he should not marry his girlfriend because she is not right for him, the quickest way to get yourself shut out (and have him upset with you, in the process) is to use the "I'm right and this is why" strategy. Forget it. It doesn't work. Instead, keep your ego in check by cultivating the ability to ask the right questions. Don't expect those questions to result in your friend saying, "You know what, I was wrong. You are right. I am not going to ask her to marry me. Thank you." However, your questions can plant seeds that may take root when your friend retreats to his mind to consider the situation. The best questions are not the ones that require "yes" or "no" answers. Rather, they are questions that get the other person thinking. There is no set of standard "get a person thinking" questions. But, if the questions come from a place that is authentic and compassionate, they will be the right ones.

The last point that I will share with you about strengthening your ability to influence and persuade is simple—pick your battles. If you challenge everyone on everything or if you go "all in" on everything, your ability to persuade when you really need to will be significantly diminished. We both know people who are constantly nit-picking. Everything is important and everything should be their way. I think of these people as shooting a BB gun. Pew! Pew! Pew! They are non-stop with their irritating and annoying BBs. The truth is that when everything is important, nothing is important. My recommendation to you is to only shoot cannonballs but with much less frequency. Gain a reputation as someone who doesn't speak often but when you do . . . boom! . . . cannonball. Learning to keep your mouth shut is one of life's most challenging lessons. I have found that when in doubt—keep your mouth shut. Of course, there are better ways to do this or that, and maybe you think your friend would like to hear all about those ways. I have learned that you can be a friend, or you can be a know-it-all, but you can't be both. An intelligent man knows what to say, a wise man knows if he should say it.

*Love,*
*Dad*

*Dear Hunter*

Of all the personal characteristics that pave the road to success, I have found that one stands above the rest—persistence. In my own words, persistence is the ability to absorb criticism, rejection, and failure and continue on towards your goal undeterred. The virtues of persistence have long been extolled by many of the greatest minds. My favorite reflection on persistence comes from America's 30th president, Calvin Coolidge. "Nothing in this world can take the place of persistence. Talent will not; nothing is more common than unsuccessful men with talent. Genius will not; unrewarded genius is almost a proverb. Education will not; the world is full of educated derelicts. Persistence and determination alone are omnipotent."

Although I have believed in the value of persistence for my entire adult life, I have admittedly been weak in practicing persistence for much of my life. I was blessed—and cursed—with a modest dose of academic and athletic talent. As a result, things came easily to me as a child and young adult. To further compound my blessing (curse), I grew up in a small town, so I quickly became a big fish in a little pond. The situation was not completely lost on me. I realized that I didn't have to work as hard in school as other people and that there was likely a long-term negative consequence associated with this that would catch up with me someday. However, persistence is like a muscle, in that awareness of a muscle's weakness does not strengthen the muscle. The persistence muscle must be used and challenged in the throes of a "struggle" in order to grow. As a result of avoiding the struggle, my persistence muscle was not strengthened until much later in life.

I would contend that the struggle related to persistence is not necessary for the sake of struggling. More specifically, if you are leveraging your talents in a way that brings you success, you should be proud of that. I do not want to instill a sense of shame in you because you derive success from your talents. If you are happy being a big fish in a small pond, there is no need to seek out the struggle. There is no need to look for opportunities to push yourself beyond your comfort zones. However, if you have a desire to rise to the top in any field, you must seek out the struggle because it is in the struggle where growth occurs. Not all, but most, of the struggle can be tackled by continuing to show up. As Woody Allen said, "Eighty percent of success is showing up." Doing so requires facing your fears of inadequacy and failure and knowing that today might not be the day you break through, but one of your tomorrows is that day, and so you must keep showing up.

I recall a Naval Officer that I served with on a fast-attack submarine that epitomized this philosophy. Mo wasn't the sharpest, smartest, or most talented officer on the submarine, but in retrospect, I realize that he was the most mentally tough among us. We used to call Mo a "weeble wobble," which is a reference to an old toy that was weighed heavily on the bottom such that you could knock the toy down, but it would, by design, get right back up. The commercial jingle for the toy, which we would often repeat about Mo, was "Weebles wobble, but they don't fall down." As an inexperienced officer, Mo would routinely get his ass handed to him by more senior officers aboard the submarine for his shortcomings. I saw Mo take verbal beatings that made me not want to step into the limelight for fear of experiencing a similar fate. Not Mo—he never backed down. He just kept showing up for the most challenging assignments. At the time, I couldn't figure out why he would do that to himself. Slowly, but surely, Mo became one of the most relied upon and respected officers on the submarine. It took a few years, but Mo had learned the hard way how to handle his business successfully. I also admired Mo's courage and persistence but could never quite match it. Admittedly, I didn't have to match Mo's persistence because the skill sets required of an officer on a submarine came easier to me. However, I always knew, in my heart of hearts, that Mo had something I didn't—and that was grit.

Grit means different things to different people, but I look at grit as a grown-up version of persistence. In my book, grit is the ability to persevere in the face of adversity in the pursuit of meaningful and long-term goals. Grit is the ability to see the big picture; life is usually a marathon and not a sprint. Truth be told, I am hardwired to be a sprinter. I tend to be impatient and pursing delayed gratification is not my strong suit. My life has generally been composed of a series of short-term pursuits that can be achieved with short and concentrated bursts of effort. However, I have learned time and again that those that reach the top of the mountain are often not the strongest or the fastest, but ones that are willing to endure failure, rejection, and pain . . . and keep showing up. I'm learning strategies for countering my sprinter's nature that I will share with you in the event that you, too, are a sprinter.

- Break big goals into small goals. A marathon doesn't have to be 26 miles. Instead, it can be 260 1/10ths of a mile. For example, writing a book is a marathon-type endeavor. If I had my way, I would finish the book in one sitting. If it required more than that, I would be unlikely to endure the price of delayed gratification. So, I break the book into a series of letters, and I record my daily progress in terms of words written. Any number of words is acceptable except zero. As long as there is progress, I'm moving in the right direction and demonstrating perseverance. This is definitely a personal preference that I don't anticipate would be useful for everyone, but if I have a long-term goal, I need a spreadsheet to track my progress. I need something to look at every day to remind me that I am making progress.

- Focus on your "why." Demonstrating persistence and grit in the face of adversity requires a fundamental reason why you are choosing to endure the struggle, the pain, and the failure. The alternative of walking away is too easy without a deeply rooted "why." Sadly, many of the most driven people that you will meet have underlying psychological issues that drive their ability to persevere. I don't wish these issues of inadequacy on anyone, but it is true. If you don't have an underlying psychosis propelling you to levels of masochism in pursuit of your dreams, you will need to explore your motivation so you can remind yourself "why" you are striving for greatness.

- Embrace hope and optimism. Some people choose to view the universe as a dangerous, unforgiving, and heartless place. We have the ability to decide to view the universe as a warm, inviting, and hopeful place. How we approach life is largely determined by how we assess the nature of the universe. As this is a choice, it is my recommendation that you learn to embrace the latter view. There is ample evidence to suggest either viewpoint is correct. If you want to see death and despair, you will see it. If you want to see life and hope, you will see it. Focus on the grand possibilities and endless opportunities that the world can provide you, and your ability to withstand bumps in the road along the journey will increase tenfold. What you are is God's gift to you; what you become is your gift to God.

- Surround yourself with people of persistence and grit. I have heard that we become the average of the five people that we spend the most time with. There is a lot of truth to this. If you want to be physically fit, hang out with physically fit people. If you want to be rich, hang out with rich people. Choose your friends and acquaintances wisely. Seek out people who will propel you to higher levels of achievement. Seek out people who demonstrate persistence and grit in their own lives.

As I reflect upon your life, I certainly hope you will be blessed with talent and that you find success as a result of this talent. However, I also hope that you have a healthy dose of "struggle" in your journey. When you encounter this struggle, please reflect on the nature of this gift, because that is what it is . . . a gift. The struggle is what builds our character and sets the stage for our success.

*Love,*
*Dad*

*Dear Hunter*

Poetry can be a snapshot into the human condition that resonates deeply with our true self. Often poetry as an art form can tickle our senses in a way that prose cannot. It has been said that poetry has the ability to communicate with our souls even before the mind can comprehend it. I agree. There is something powerful about a poem that touches you in ways that you can't quite comprehend. You will undoubtedly find poems that can help carry you through the vicissitudes of your life. The three poems that follow were those for me. I've had these poems taped to my desk as I studied nuclear physics in college, on my rack on a nuclear submarine, and tucked in my wallet for decades.

***

## Desiderata by Max Ehrmann

Go placidly amid the noise and the haste, and remember what peace there may be in silence. As far as possible, without surrender, be on good terms with all persons.

Speak your truth quietly and clearly; and listen to others, even to the dull and the ignorant; they too have their story.

Avoid loud and aggressive persons; they are vexatious to the spirit. If you compare yourself with others, you may become vain or bitter, for always there will be greater and lesser persons than yourself.

Enjoy your achievements as well as your plans. Keep interested in your own career, however humble; it is a real possession in the changing fortunes of time.

Exercise caution in your business affairs, for the world is full of trickery. But let this not blind you to what virtue there is; many persons strive for high ideals, and everywhere life is full of heroism.

Be yourself. Especially do not feign affection. Neither be cynical about love; for in the face of all aridity and disenchantment it is as perennial as the grass.

Take kindly the counsel of the years, gracefully surrendering the things of youth.

Nurture strength of spirit to shield you in sudden misfortune. But do not distress yourself with dark imaginings. Many fears are born of fatigue and loneliness.

Beyond a wholesome discipline, be gentle with yourself. You are a child of the universe no less than the trees and the stars; you have a right to be here.

And whether or not it is clear to you, no doubt the universe is unfolding as it should. Therefore be at peace with God, whatever you conceive Him to be. And whatever your labors and aspirations, in the noisy confusion of life, keep peace in your soul. With all its sham, drudgery and broken dreams, it is still a beautiful world. Be cheerful. Strive to be happy.

\*\*\*

## If by Rudyard Kipling

If you can keep your head when all about you
   Are losing theirs and blaming it on you,
If you can trust yourself when all men doubt you,
   But make allowance for their doubting too;

If you can wait and not be tired by waiting,
  Or being lied about, don't deal in lies,
Or being hated, don't give way to hating,
  And yet don't look too good, nor talk too wise:
If you can dream—and not make dreams your master;
  If you can think—and not make thoughts your aim;
If you can meet with Triumph and Disaster
  And treat those two impostors just the same;
If you can bear to hear the truth you've spoken
  Twisted by knaves to make a trap for fools,
Or watch the things you gave your life to, broken,
  And stoop and build 'em up with wornout tools:
If you can make one heap of all your winnings
  And risk it on one turn of pitch-and-toss,
And lose, and start again at your beginnings
  And never breathe a word about your loss;
If you can force your heart and nerve and sinew
  To serve your turn long after they are gone,
And so hold on when there is nothing in you
  Except the Will which says to them: 'Hold on!'
If you can talk with crowds and keep your virtue,
  Or walk with Kings—nor lose the common touch,
If neither foes nor loving friends can hurt you;
  If all men count with you, but none too much;
If you can fill the unforgiving minute
With sixty seconds' worth of distance run,

Yours is the Earth and everything that's in it,
And—which is more—you'll be a Man, my son!

\*\*\*

Stopping by Woods on a Snowy Evening by Robert Frost

Whose woods these are I think I know.
His house is in the village though;
He will not see me stopping here
To watch his woods fill up with snow.

My little horse must think it queer
To stop without a farmhouse near
Between the woods and frozen lake
The darkest evening of the year.

He gives his harness bells a shake
To ask if there is some mistake.
The only other sound's the sweep
Of easy wind and downy flake.

The woods are lovely, dark and deep,
But I have promises to keep,
And miles to go before I sleep,
And miles to go before I sleep.

*Love,*

*Dad*

*Dear Hunter*

Demonstrating the appropriate amount of confidence in life is a tricky endeavor. On one hand, under confidence can paralyze you and prevent you from tackling life's most challenging and rewarding opportunities. On the other hand, overconfidence can easily bleed into arrogance, which can make you a social pariah in the blink of an eye. Striking the balance between these two ends of the spectrum is a challenge that I have spent my life attempting to achieve.

Before delving into a discussion about confidence, we should probably take a moment to think about what confidence is. Confidence, as a personality trait, is the self-assuredness that comes from a belief in one's abilities to handle the challenges or threats an environment presents. Using this definition, we see that confidence is not just about how we feel about our abilities, but it is also a reflection of our assessment of the challenges or threats in our environment. This highlights a common misconception about confidence. Often, people assume confidence is a reflection of a person's self-esteem. This certainly can be true. However, I have found that more often than not, a crisis of confidence is related to how a person perceives the challenges and threats in his environment.

Author Charles Bukowski said, "The problem with the world is that the intelligent people are full of doubts, while the stupid ones are full of confidence." The insightful paradox of this quote makes me smile. While I agree with Bukowski's assessment at a surface level, let's explore why this quote seems to be both illogical and true. Intelligent people, or perhaps more accurately, thoughtful people, are more likely to thoroughly assess a situation or environment than those who are less thoughtful. Further, intelligent people are more likely to identify threats and potential pitfalls in a situation. As a result, they may be more timid, careful, or even hesitant in their environment than their less intelligent or thoughtful peers. However, most of the threats that we identify in life never actually manifest. As Mark Twain said, "I have been through some terrible things in my life, some of which actually happened." Sure, it is possible that you may be surrounded by a pack of wild animals in your backyard, but the likelihood is that you won't be. Therefore, the less intelligent people blissfully, if not ignorantly, bumble their way forward, while the thoughtful people tend to be more prone to paralysis because of all the "what-ifs" circulating in their minds.

Often in my life, I have found myself figuratively staring at a map of the road ahead of me while standing still. The map is populated with all the obstacles and pitfalls that I envision on that road. I'm stuck in my tracks because the challenges seem overwhelming, or at least worthy of consideration. Meanwhile, my counterparts blow right by me because they either don't see the same obstacles that I do or aren't worried about them. Over time, more action trumps less action, and the "ignorant" folks move further down the road, while I'm stuck staring at the map. In this context, the lack of confidence is not a reflection of the assessment of my abilities, but rather an assessment of the challenges that my abilities will have to tackle. Additionally, there is an issue of standards to consider. If you are an "A" student, your confidence level is likely to be based on your assessed ability to achieve a figurative "A" in any life endeavor. This is the "A-student trap" because outside of your formal education, there are no assigned grades and life does not reward us for having an "A" answer to all of life's challenges. I have witnessed first-hand how this phenomenon can impact an "A" student's confidence level in tackling life challenges. Sometimes good is good enough. Don't let your confidence be buried beneath an artificially inflated standard of performance.

After spending years wrestling with this topic, I've learned a few things that have helped me to develop a more balanced approach to confidence in my day-to-day life. For starters, there is nothing wrong with having a mental map of pitfalls and challenges. That is a thoughtful way to approach life. However, I've learned that I can't let those concerns stop me from moving forward. Sometimes it means I may not be sprinting through a field of landmines, but it does mean that I keep moving forward. As Martin Luther King, Jr. said, "If you can't fly then run, if you can't run then walk, if you can't walk then crawl, but whatever you do you have to keep moving forward." I believe it is okay to let your confidence level act as a throttle to the speed at which you pursue your goals, but never as a brake.

Further, confidence is not a binary personality trait. Instead, confidence is very contextual. There is acute confidence and general confidence, and it is my observation that these two types are often confused for one another. Acute confidence relates to a specific task or environment. For example, some people may be confident on the dance floor, in the boardroom, or at the gym. This type of confidence relates to your comfort in a very specific arena of life. Acute confidence comes from experience. You would be hard-pressed to convince me that I should be confident wrestling an alligator as I have no experience in doing so. In contrast, general confidence is the confidence that someone exudes in the context of life . . . generally. I think of general confidence as a baseline that we carry through all environments. It is reflective of our assessment of our general abilities to handle life. Acute confidence either adds or subtracts to that baseline, depending upon your environment.

Be careful of how you value other people. You will have a tendency to value highly confident people above less confident people. This is natural, but it is a tendency that must be acknowledged and often curbed. Life is so full of uncertainty that when we run across someone who is teeming with confidence, we are likely to feel drawn to them because we may, at some level, want to believe that maybe they have life "figured out." Of course, this does not imply that you should hold people's confidence against them, but it does mean that you should approach highly confident people with a grain of suspicion. Never forget that the expression "con man" is short for "confidence man." These hooligans rely on their ability to gain your trust by exuding high levels of confidence. Don't be lured into their gravitational pull by the words they use. Instead, hold your judgment based on their actions. As Ralph Waldo Emerson said, "What you do speaks so loudly that I cannot hear what you say."

The confidence you exude will directly impact how others perceive you. If you are overconfident, you will immediately turn people off. If you are under confident, people will label you as weak or submissive. How do you find the right balance? For starters, learn to establish a confidence level that is based on your true feelings and not on what you believe other people's expectations to be. One surefire way to lose the superpower of authenticity is to mold your personality to the perceived desires of others. It is a losing strategy because a harsh reality of life is that you will never make everyone happy. When it comes to confidence, you can be sure that there will be people who label you as arrogant from time to time, and there will be people who label you as weak from time to time. What other people think of you is none of your business.

Learn to cultivate what is often described as quiet confidence. Quiet confidence is not boastful or arrogant. It is neither meek nor submissive. Instead, quiet confidence is the personality trait that naturally follows from being comfortable in your skin. This may take many years to develop, but I adamantly believe it is one of the most fundamental traits that leads to success, peace of mind, and the respect of others. Quiet confidence means:

- You have the courage to speak up for what you believe in, but also have the humility to accept that you may be wrong.

- You are striving to be your best self and have given up the losing strategy of comparing yourself to others.

- You are willing to take risks in life, but you also accept the consequences of those risks, good or bad, without blaming others.

- Although you are comfortable taking center stage in pursuit of your ambitions, you do not need the limelight to validate your worth.

- You are authentically "you" and proud, without being boastful, of your abilities, achievements, and dreams.

If I could wish that you be remembered as one descriptor, right behind "kind," I would choose "quietly confident."

*Love,*
*Dad*

*Dear Hunter*

The existential question, "Who am I?" will likely absorb a substantial amount of your mental resources over your lifetime. There are many lenses through which to view this question. There is the spiritual lens where you may find yourself questioning who you are in the greater context of time and space. There is the external lens where you may question how others perceive you. There is an internal lens where you may consider how you perceive yourself. Dissecting this question has kept philosophers busy for centuries. Pragmatically, I would offer for your consideration that you are your actions. More specifically, I would contend that you are your actions that you routinely perform—your habits. Ultimately, your habits become your character. I agree with Tony Robbins who once said, "In essence, if we want to direct our lives, we must take control of our consistent actions. It's not what we do once in a while that shapes our lives, but what we do consistently."

Consider a person who when asked, "Who are you?" responds that they are kind and compassionate. Would it be reasonable to ask this person what do they do that is kind and compassionate? If they had trouble answering this question, is it fair to say that they may not be as kind and compassionate as they think they are? We often develop a mental construct of our identity that reflects who we want to be rather than who we are. For example, you know people that you would describe as rude and obnoxious. Do you think that they would describe themselves as rude and obnoxious? Probably not. Why not? Among other reasons, most people view themselves through an internal lens and that lens is biased towards who they want to be, not necessarily who they are. The "who we actually are" lens is focused almost exclusively on our actions—not our intentions, our desires, or our internal lens of who we want to be.

Modifying our actions to fit our view of ourselves is much easier said than done. Our habits become hardwired into our brains and modifying them can be a daunting task. When I retired from the military, my lifestyle changed drastically. One of those changes was my physical fitness and health. In a matter of a few years I gained 40 pounds, was in the worst shape of my life, and my dietary habits were horrible. Several times I committed myself to changing my lifestyle, and several times I failed. I was motivated to change. I had established a plan of action that included meal preparation and a workout regime. Within a few days, I was back to my unhealthy habits. This story is not unique to my experiences. Every year, people establish New Year's resolutions, and every year people lapse into their old habits before the calendar flips to February. Why? Why is it so challenging to change a habit? There are many theories in the fields of psychology and neurology that are available for consumption if you are so inclined to delve into this topic. However, I believe I have a loophole that you can use to change any habit. That loophole is simple: Make your adjustment so small and manageable that you couldn't possibly fail.

For example, when I found myself failing to replace my bad habits of physical fitness and health with more productive habits, I stumbled upon this loophole. Out of desperation I decided to make myself a promise to do one pushup a day. That's right, just one pushup a day. I further promised myself that I wouldn't even attempt to modify my diet or go to the gym until I had successfully performed one pushup a day for 30 consecutive days. I do not recall why I thought such a meager goal would be an effective way to get back into shape, but I stumbled into a powerful method that yielded amazing results. The principle behind these results is not that much different from the principle governing why a river can carve through a mountain. A river carves through a mountain not through brute force, but through the sustained application of a small amount of pressure.

The manner in which the one pushup a day habit played out was quite remarkable. The first few days were as you would expect— ordinary. Of course, I didn't just do one pushup a day because the real work of doing pushups is carving out the time and getting into the pushup position, and once that was done, I was more inclined to do five or more pushups. What I discovered over the first week was that I was making slightly better decisions in my day-to-day life. I would do a few pushups which got my blood flowing a bit, and then when I went to the refrigerator to get a drink, I selected water instead of soda. Drinking water instead of soda increased my hydration slightly. As a result of being more hydrated and less caffeinated, I slept slightly better at night. Sleeping slightly better at night allowed me to wake up a bit earlier and in a slightly better mood. This allowed me the opportunity to spend a few minutes meditating before work. Meditating for a few minutes before work resulted in a slightly more pleasant workday. Therefore, when I came home, I felt motivated to do a few more pushups, which inspired me to eat a slightly healthier dinner.

The cycle continued with incremental but sustainable progress. After having performed this routine for about three weeks, where the only requirement was to do at least one pushup a day, I was out running some errands when I saw a boxing gym. I had seen this gym before and was intrigued but didn't have the gumption to go inside and see what the gym had to offer. However, that day was different. I had just enough motivation to step inside and inquire about the gym. The next morning, I was taking a boxing class. Fast forward to four months later, I had dropped 30 pounds and was in great shape. My diet had dramatically changed for the better. I felt healthy for the first time in a long time. And it all started with a commitment to do one pushup a day. As Mark Twain said, "Habit is habit and not to be flung out of the window by any man, but coaxed downstairs a step at a time."

A necessary part of developing new habits is creating a pre-planned response for dealing with setbacks. For example, assume you aspire to do one pushup a day for 30 consecutive days. One day 15, you fail to do so. Now what? For many people what should be a small setback turns into a failure. How? They fail to do the pushup on day

16 because they convince themselves that they will start again at the beginning of next month, which is only five days away. But next month comes and goes. I'd like to tell you that this is uncommon, but my experience teaches me that it is more common than not. People routinely allow small setbacks to completely derail their progress towards their goals. When embarking on forming habits, make yourself a promise. *I will not suffer a setback two days in a row.* If you can abide by this one simple rule, the chances of failing drop to near zero. Remember, setbacks are not failures unless they result in you giving up. As Winston Churchill said, "This is the lesson: never give in, never give in, never, never, never, never—in nothing, great or small, large or petty—never give in except to convictions of honour and good sense."

Your goals and ambitions are best served by matching habits to desires; often, people will instead match outcomes with desires. For example, assume that you have an ambition to become a *New York Times* bestselling author. It may feel natural to tie this goal to an outcome. Specifically, writing a book worthy of this achievement. That is a daunting task that has the potential to overwhelm your mind and stagnate your efforts. *When will I have the time to perform such a task? Am I a good enough writer to do so?* Instead, I encourage you to consider answering the following question: What might the likely habits of a bestselling author be? One such habit may be the willingness to write everyday no matter their motivational level. Seek to establish this habit and distance yourself emotionally from the end state. We become our habits, so establish your habit wisely and feel free to "steal" from others.

*Love,*
*Dad*

*Dear Hunter*

I hope that this letter does not apply to you. Procrastination is a vile demon, and I hope that he is not genetic. The roots of procrastination are interwoven with a plethora of emotions, but the most prevalent one is fear. Procrastination is the symptom, and fear is the disease. Often, perfectionism is at the heart of this fear. Fear of being labeled a fraud, looking foolish, or being useless. The most critical thing to understand about procrastination is that it is reflective of an emotional struggle, not a time management struggle. Further, it is self-sabotaging behavior. Those of us that wrestle with the demon of procrastination are under no delusions about its destructive nature.

Procrastination is an emotionally charged defense mechanism that attempts to delay, indefinitely, the realization that somehow you are less than. This illogical behavior assumes, at some level, that if you don't go into the forest, the monster can't get you. Unfortunately, the monster gets stronger and stronger with each passing day that you don't enter the forest and eventually tracks you down.

The consequences of procrastination can range from minor to life-altering. I have personally felt the full range of these consequences throughout my life. Chronic procrastination can rob you of opportunities to become a better person. My first recollection of procrastinating in a manner that robbed me of a significant life opportunity occurred in my freshman year of high school. For World History class we were assigned a year-long project. The project was to find a current event from the newspaper each day and write a few sentences about it in a journal. I remember thinking this was a really cool idea. However, my perfectionism got the best of me. Since the project wasn't "due" until the end of the year, I delayed taking action. I was collecting newspapers in my bedroom for the first few weeks of the school year, thinking that I would catch up eventually.

Weeks turned into months, and, before I knew it, I had only a few days left until we had to turn in our journals. I had nothing written. I confessed to my parents about what I had done and asked if I could take a day off from school and spend the day at the public library doing the project. They allowed me to do so. I spent 12 hours at the library hastily combing through the last year's newspapers and jotting down a few sentences on each event. I completed the project, but I robbed myself of an opportunity to develop a great habit of keeping up with current events. Further, I robbed myself of an opportunity to learn that not every assignment is a sprint; the most satisfying work more closely resembles a marathon. I didn't foster an appreciation for the satisfaction that could be gained by taking a project one step at a time and one day at a time until much later in life.

Procrastination can impact not only our academic and professional lives, but also our relationships. You will find throughout your life that there are things that you want to share with people that you are close with. An example may include telling a family member how much you love them, thanking a teacher or coach for the life lessons they taught you, or telling a friend whom you have grown apart from that you still think of them often and dearly. Sharing emotional or intimate sentiments can be difficult. I will tell you that what is even more difficult is missing out on the opportunity to do so. I've left things unsaid to my grandparents, some teachers and coaches, and to friends, and it is now too late to do so. Everyone you know will eventually pass away. I beg you not to let your thoughts remain caged inside of you because you procrastinated in sharing them with their intended recipient.

The procrastination tendency followed me for a good part of my life and I still wrestle with this demon from time to time. I have tried many different tactics to overcome my own procrastination with varying degrees of success. Like many struggles in life, intellectually understanding the problem and emotionally addressing the problem are often worlds apart. However, that does not mean that having a tendency towards procrastination is a life sentence; what it does mean is that you will need to learn effective strategies for overcoming procrastination if and when you are afflicted with it.

Years ago, I experienced a breakthrough that has helped me overcome my proclivity for procrastination. It was a Saturday afternoon on a cold winter's day. I had very little to do and nowhere to be. I was folding laundry—one of my least favorite chores. I reduced the size of a mountainous pile of recently cleaned clothes one article at a time. I grabbed a white undershirt and began to fold it. The T-shirt was inside-out. I hesitated before folding it. Should I fix it? I held and stared at the T-shirt as I contemplated turning it right side out. Truth be told, I could have righted the T-shirt four times in the span that I contemplated what to do. But I was no longer thinking about the T-shirt, my mind shifted into a philosophical mode.

*Someone is going to fix this T-shirt. It's either going to be me or my future self. One of us is going to do it, and I get to choose.*

That doesn't seem very fair to the future me—he gets no vote in this? The choice was obvious. It's a lazy Saturday afternoon, and I have nothing pressing on my plate. My future self is undoubtedly going to be running five minutes late for work when he grabs this shirt. Which one of us should tackle this? No brainer, right? But that's not how those of us with the procrastination bug roll. We are selfish and disrespectful to our future selves.

Time is the most precious commodity in our lives, and it is limited. Piling up crappy tasks on my future self who is always rushing to leave the house on time seems like a poor decision. He's the guy whom I am counting on to achieve my dreams, maybe I should be working harder at freeing up his time so that he can get moving on that.

My new anti-procrastination pep talk is: *Don't be so freaking selfish. Show your future self the same level of respect you would show anyone that you loved.*

Another tactic for overcoming procrastination is to follow the advice of Mark Twain, who recommended: "Eat a live frog first thing in the morning and nothing worse will happen to you the rest of the day." Develop a habit of "eating a frog" to start your day, and you will be well on your way to overcoming procrastination. Recall that you are your habits. Procrastination is not about delaying all work. Procrastination is about delaying undesirable work like eating a live frog. Therefore, make a habit of performing the most uncomfortable work on your plate as your first act of the day. This habit, like all habits, is difficult to develop but with persistence and consistency, it can help keep the procrastination monster at bay.

The journey of a thousand miles begins with a single step. Often the perfectionist inside of me is fearful of the journey. *A thousand miles?! How could I possibly travel a thousand miles?* As a result, the journey never starts. Worse, it is not as if I make a conscious decision to forego the journey. At least that decision has some finality to it. Instead, the procrastinator tells himself that they will absolutely embark upon the journey, but just not today. For the chronic procrastinator, today is never the day because on some level, they never feel prepared for the journey. I implore you to approach every journey as a series of individual steps. If you are feeling overwhelmed and find yourself procrastinating, please think of this letter and simply take one step. Every challenge, no matter how large or complex, can be broken into a smaller series of steps. Identify those steps and take the first one. After you take that first step, regardless of how small it may be—take a deep breath, congratulate yourself, and then take the next step. Overnight success stories usually consist of ten-plus years of taking one step at a time. Be brave and enter the forest!

I have more to share with you about procrastination, but I'll write the rest of this letter later . . .

*Love,*
*Dad*

*Dear Hunter*

Admittedly and somewhat embarrassingly, I've spent the better part of my life chasing happiness without a clear grasp of what exactly that means. It may seem odd to chase something fervently without a clear understanding of what you are chasing, but I don't think that I am alone. "I just want to be happy" is a battle cry of millions, but what exactly does that even mean? What is happiness? As Yogi Berra said, "If you don't know where you are going, you might wind up someplace else."

Having spent the better part of two decades contemplating the meaning of happiness, I would contend that the word *happiness* has three distinct meanings, which are often confused for one another. In each case, the word *happy* means feeling a sense of pleasure or contentment but in three unique ways: happiness as a short-term emotion, happiness as a descriptor for your place in life, and happiness as a reflection of your peace of mind. Let's talk about each of these contexts and then we'll discuss how they inter-relate.

Happiness as a short-term emotion is the most common connotation of the word happy, as in, "You don't look happy today" or, "I am so happy it is sunny today." Your short-term emotions ebb and flow like the tide. You will have moments of happiness, sadness, anger, and boredom, among others. If you expect to be happy all of the time in this context, you can expect to be disappointed. Many people mistakenly use this context as their singular definition of what it means to live a happy life. Although you can and should seek out environments, activities, and people that make you feel happy, this is the most fleeting of the three concepts of happiness. It is appropriate to appreciate the full range of emotions that you experience. Moreover, I highly encourage you to bask in the simple pleasures of life when they present themselves to you. However, it is errant to associate living a happy life exclusively with this fleeting happiness. I have seen those of the "if it feels good, do it" crowd seek out temporary short-term happiness at the expense of longer-term happiness, and they spend their lives chasing a ghost.

Happiness as a descriptor for your place in life can be more stable than the short-term emotion of happiness. You can be happy (or unhappy) with your job, your relationships, or your hobbies. This type of happiness often is not accompanied by the joy or bliss associated with short-term emotional happiness, but it has a powerful impact on your satisfaction with your life. As we consider different types of happiness, we can highlight the confusion that can sometimes result. For example, assume that you are living a satisfying life that you worked hard to create for yourself. On a rainy day, you are driving to work and a raccoon darts in front of your car. You swerve to avoid the raccoon and in doing so you spill your piping hot cup of coffee on your shirt and tie. Additionally, your car's tires hit the curb and you flatten a tire. You exit the car, covered in coffee, to examine the flat tire. You check your watch; you have an important meeting that starts in 30 minutes. You are definitely going to be late. If we pause life in this instant and ask you, "Are you happy?" chances are you would not respond in the affirmative. Does this mean you are an unhappy person? Well, in one sense of the word *happiness*, the short-term emotion type, this would be true. You are not happy. The converse is true as well. I can recall times in my life where I was very dissatisfied with my lot in life and generally unhappy. Even in those times a well-timed joke, a New York Yankees' win, or a good cup of coffee could make me temporarily happy.

Happiness as a reflection of your peace of mind is achieved when you make peace with your existence and your place in the universe. Peace of mind is my lifelong ambition above all others. In my opinion, this is the truest form of happiness. At the core of a peaceful mind is an optimistic and grateful mindset. I believe that you will find that there is always a reason to be happy if you are so inclined to look for it. Conversely, there is always a reason to be unhappy. This doesn't mean that you will not experience the emotion of unhappiness in the form of sadness, frustration, or anger. It means that after the wave of emotion is felt and acknowledged, you have the ability to choose happiness. It is my observation that people are generally as happy as they choose to be. If you can achieve a peaceful mind imbued with optimism and gratitude, you will find that the other forms of happiness will follow.

Although I've presented these three types of happiness as distinct entities, it is clear that they are very much related. However, I thought it was appropriate to point out their separateness to help you evaluate your own levels of happiness as they relate to decisions that you will make. For example, you will often have to sacrifice short-term happiness for longer-term happiness. Although I believe this to be true, I hesitate to say it because I've seen so many people forego happiness today for their vision of happiness tomorrow. Often, tomorrow never comes for these people. I don't want to see you fall into this trap. Pragmatically, however, you may find yourself from time to time having to sacrifice short-term happiness to build the life that you desire. These sacrifices may take the form of foregoing sleep or social activities to dedicate yourself to an academic or professional endeavor that will pay dividends in the future.

There are a few other happiness traps that I'd like to share with you:

- Following other people's ideas of happiness. A fundamental truth about happiness is that happiness is uniquely defined for every person who has ever walked the planet. There is nothing more unfulfilling than to scrape, scratch, and claw for a dream that is not yours. You will experience times of confusion and doubt when there is a disconnect between your idea of happiness and the guidance from those whose opinions you hold dear. Learn to appreciate and absorb this guidance, but ultimately learn to follow the beat of your drum.

- Assuming that happiness comes from external sources. Happiness is fueled internally. You must learn to be happy in the comfort of your skin before any relationship, job, or possession can add to your happiness. Do not ever rely on someone else for your own happiness. Doing so is not only unfair to the other person, it is a recipe for a failed relationship. You may find that other people, places, and things add to your baseline level of happiness, but do not ever let those external sources define you or your happiness.

- Assuming that you should always be happy. Emotions, like the weather, come and go. Sometimes it is wise to learn to dance in the rain and other times it is wise to hunker down on the couch and watch movies until the storm passes. Without the valleys of life, we wouldn't appreciate the mountaintops. In the challenging times, remind yourself that this too shall pass.

- Forgetting about the happiness of others. We do, in fact, reap what we sow. It is common for people to become so absorbed in achieving their own happiness that they neglect the importance of sowing happiness in the lives of others. In fact, I would contend that when the days get dark, the quickest way to find the sunshine is to shift your focus to others. What can you do to help? What can you do to make someone else happy? The universe has an uncanny habit of delivering the energy that we share with the world back to us.

I've observed the spread of so much misinformation about happiness that I thought it would be valuable to take a step back and consider the different types of happiness that are often combined into one confusing clump. However, I don't want to give you the impression that happiness is something to evaluate logically like a calculus equation. Ultimately, you will need to trust your gut instinct to guide your path. Often, happiness is simply a descriptor for an awareness and appreciation of the beauty of life. This mindset can manifest itself in your ability to appreciate fresh fallen snow, a hot slice of pizza, a starry night sky, or even the wonders of quantum physics. Happiness is a choice. You will be as happy as you choose to be.

More than anything, I wish that you will live a life filled with happiness and joy—however you choose to define those terms. There is no close second on my list of wishes for you.

*Love,*
*Dad*

*Dear Hunter*

Yesterday, we had a big snowstorm in Chicago. I bundled you up in your snow pants, boots, jacket, hat, and gloves, and we walked around the neighborhood. I watched with amazement and joy as you played in the snow with reckless abandon for hours. I was doing my best to embrace every second of it because I know how fleeting this time with you is. Today you are a two-and-a-half-year old toddler but soon, likely before I know it, you will be a man. I'd like you to read this letter on July 20, 2036. You will have just turned 18 years old. Wow! I can hardly believe this day will come! But I know it will; the passage of time is relentless.

Your late teen years are a turning point in your life. For most of your life, you have relied upon me and your mother to provide you with food, shelter, and comfort. You are embarking on a period of your life where you are no longer dependent on us for survival. Your mind is formulating ideas that are uniquely your own. Your hopes and dreams are developing faster and in a more tangible way than they ever have before. You are truly becoming your own man. Please know that I am very proud of the man you have become.

However, I also know that you are entering a stage of your life during which you will not be particularly receptive to advice from your parents. Why is this? I have no idea, but I was once 18 years old too, and although I recall loving my parents deeply, I was of the mindset that they didn't really understand me and my place in the world. I'm not sure that I would have expressed my feelings quite that way, but in retrospect, I realize that is how I felt. Contributing to this sentiment is the fact that at this age most of us still feel like a child when we're around our parents, yet the world is starting to make us feel more like an adult. This creates a split identity that can be confusing. A consequence of this split identity is to lean away from your parents as you lean into the world. As much as I'd like you to know that you don't have to lean away from us to lean into the world, I know this is probably unrealistic of me. I do, however, want to do everything I can to reach out to you and support you as you enter the world of adulthood. Here are some bits of advice that I'd like to share with you.

- We are as much your parents today as we were on the day that you were born. Our relationship will change as we age, but the unconditional love and support that you received from us as an infant is no less today or tomorrow. You can always count on us to be in your corner—no matter what. We know life is messy and we know that you are imperfect, so please never feel ashamed or embarrassed to come to us with your adult problems. The chances are good that we've had similar, if not worse, problems.

- You don't know everything . . . and you never will. I know it feels like you've got the world figured out. It is an empowering feeling; I remember it well. The reality is that most of what you think about the world today will change over time. Further, the older you get, the less you will know . . . and that is a good thing. Really?! Yes, really. I sometimes tease that I wish I were 18 again because I knew everything back then.

- Be respectful and kind to everyone you meet. It is a winning strategy and the right thing to do. As you are finding yourself, you may be tempted to establish your place in the world by pushing others down. Resist this temptation at all costs.

- Life goes on beyond your early twenties. I remember being in a rush to get my life together before I graduated from college. Finding the right field of study, the perfect partner, the right place to live. If you are feeling similar pressure, relax. Life goes on. Life is a marathon, not a sprint. Do not rush into anything, even if you are watching your friends do so. Enjoy your youthful age, and don't ruin it by placing undue pressures on yourself.

- Like it or not, you are the average of the five people whom you spend the most time with. Choose these people wisely.

- Stay open to new life experiences and activities. At your age, you likely feel that you have a good handle on your likes and dislikes as well as your talents. Be careful about allowing this assumption to become an obstacle to learning new things. I was 42 years old the first time that I picked up a paintbrush (outside of art class in grammar school) and found that I love to paint. There is no reason to wait until your 40s to explore new opportunities. Stay open to the world and all of its possibilities. Become a lifelong learner at a young age.

- Be interesting and humble. Social interactions at your age are tricky. You are only learning how to meet new people, but the number of people that you meet, or can meet, will probably never be higher. This can be stressful. I have observed that everyone your age will be looking for an angle to distinguish themselves from their peers. Chances are you will search for this angle as well. Some people choose to create a persona of the cool kid, or the jock, or the scholar, or the funny guy. Above all, be yourself. However, if you can create a persona, choose to be interesting. How? Read diverse books and magazines, have an eclectic taste in friends, food, and music, travel when you can, listen to other people's stories, and learn to adopt thinking as a hobby. Strive to be interesting, not popular. However, the necessary ingredient to combine with *interesting* is *humility*. Let other people discover that you are interesting; don't shove it down their throats.

- Nothing good happens after 2 a.m. Truth be told, the chances of getting yourself into trouble exponentially increase after midnight. Enjoy yourself and have a good time but be very careful about the decisions that you make after midnight.

- Beware of consuming alcohol. If you choose to drink socially, be known as a moderate drinker. There will always be the person at the party who dances naked on the table. Don't be that person. There will always be the person at the party that wants to start a fight. Don't be that person. There will always be the person at the party that vomits in the living room and passes out in the corner. Don't be that person. There is no valor or virtue in being that person—none—so don't be. My advice to you is to stick with beer and wine only. If you choose to drink whiskey or vodka socially in your 30s or beyond, feel free. However, you can help protect yourself from yourself if you keep hard liquor out of your hand at your age. Also, just like nothing good happens after 2 a.m., nothing good happens after someone yells, "Shots!!" Make that your time to exit.

- Nobody is judging you. Well, nobody is judging you to the extent that you think they are. I know it feels like they are, but the reality is that everyone, especially at your age, is so wrapped up in their own issues that any judgment that they are passing on others is more about their own insecurities than you. I know this sounds like a typical old-man thing to say, but it is so true. Trust me. I can't tell you how many life opportunities and experiences that I passed up, and regret, because I was worried about what people would think of me. Most of the people whose opinions you are worried about today won't even be a part of your life five years from now. Forget them. Be you.

- The world doesn't revolve around you. As a teenager, this is likely to fall on deaf ears. Why? I have no idea. The answer probably relates to the details of your social development; however, please take the time to consider your actions and what impact they will have on others. This is true throughout your life, but it is especially important at your age because you will have a tendency, whether you realize it or not, to develop tunnel vision. Specifically, by viewing your actions as they affect you, and you alone.

- Think big. Do not fear your talents and your callings. In her book *A Return to Love*, Marianne Williamson hit the nail on the head when she wrote, "Our deepest fear is not that we are inadequate. Our deepest fear is that we are powerful beyond measure. It is our light, not our darkness that most frightens us. We ask ourselves, 'Who am I to be brilliant, gorgeous, talented, fabulous?' Actually, who are you not to be? You are a child of God. Your playing small does not serve the world."

Above all, know that I am proud of you, Hunter. I am proud of the boy you are today as I write this, and I am absolutely sure I will be proud of the man you will have become when you are reading this. I love you.

*Love,*
*Dad*

*Dear Hunter*

When I was in school, I believed that education was my number one priority. My parents had their professional jobs, and my job was my schooling. I took that responsibility very seriously. I graduated at the top of my middle school and high school class and earned a full academic scholarship to college. Anyone who knew me in high school knew that I was as serious about school, if not more so, as anyone else. My heart was in the right place, but there was a fundamental truth about education that I did not grasp until later in life. That truth is that learning is more critical than grades. Grades are important, don't get me wrong, but your priority as a student should be to learn. I didn't grasp this when I was in school, and I wish I had. I would contend that your grades will follow suit if your focus is learning, but the converse is not necessarily true.

Although our education system affords you unlimited opportunities to strengthen your mind, formal education elements can be impediments to your future development. If I could go back to school, I would approach my education differently based on what I now understand to be true about education. I would like to share some of those lessons with you.

The number one skill that your formal education will teach you is learning how to learn. Let's face it; you will forget most of the details about what you are taught and tested on in your formal education. As Albert Einstein said, "Education is what remains after one has forgotten what one has learned in school." How do you optimize your "education" in learning how to learn?

Take nothing at face value. Ponder the material deeply, ask questions, and then carefully consider the answers you get to those questions. In time you will learn how to ask questions effectively. You want to avoid being the student in class with a million questions while also avoiding being the student who is fearful of asking questions. Resist the temptation to ask questions as a means of demonstrating your knowledge. As you develop this skill, follow your authentic self for guidance. In my professional career, I would rank the ability to ask insightful and thought-provoking questions as the number one skill set needed for professional development, achievement, and advancement.

Recognize when you are being taught how to use a tool versus being taught an application. If you were being trained to be a carpenter, you would first need to learn how to use a hammer before building a staircase. Often, I've seen students lament and resist learning how to use tools, asking, as students have been asking for generations, "When will I ever have to use this in my life?!" Don't be so short-sighted. Calculus is a tool, but rocket science is an application that has put men on the moon. Grammar is a tool, but persuasive writing is an application that can change the hearts and minds of millions. Accounting is a tool, but entrepreneurship is an application that can change the world. Without the tools, the applications would not be possible. Learn to appreciate the craft of working with tools, and you will reap the benefits of their application further down the road.

Become outstanding at developing analogies. Memorization may help you ace a test on Thursday but producing an analogy for new information will help you learn and retain this new information. This skill allows you to leverage the knowledge that you already possess to absorb, digest, and retain new information with less effort. For example, many students struggle to understand the concept and application of electricity. I have found the topic much more palpable if I think about running water through pipes instead of electrons through wires. The concepts such as voltage, resistance, and current can be thought of as water pressure, pipe size and flow rate, which are more intuitive. An added benefit of learning with analogies is that you will drastically improve your ability to describe these topics to someone unfamiliar with them. Someone who can effectively communicate new and critical concepts is invaluable in the workplace. Outside of a formal education environment, it is rarely enough to know something. You must be able to share that knowledge.

Formal education provides countless benefits and opportunities. However, the classroom is not a perfect replication of the world outside of the classroom. Although teachers and administrators strive valiantly to create an environment that will translate to success outside of school, it is impossible and unrealistic to expect their efforts to be perfect. Here are some instances where the "real world" strays from the academic world.

- There is rarely a syllabus in the real world. The luxury of formal education is the relative black-and-white nature of the student's and teacher's expectations. Before the semester, the teacher lays out the assignments, required readings, test dates, and grading criteria. There is no such luxury outside of the classroom. Although there are still expectations, requirements, and grading, they are much less formal and presented with much more uncertainty. I have seen this uncertainty drive people nuts because they cannot let go of the classroom's certainty. Enjoy the luxury while you can, but do not get too used to it.

- There is rarely partial credit in the real world. Consider a fifth-grade test question: "Name two facts about George Washington" (2 pts). Little Billy's answer is:
  1. He was the first president of the United States.
  2. He was a traveling circus clown named Bobo.

- How many points is Billy awarded? One point? Probably. Thirteen years later, Billy's boss asks him a question. Billy doesn't know the answer and now has a choice. He can say, "I don't know, but I will find out," or he can spew random bull crap and hope that some of it is true. If he chooses the latter, he may be suffering from a case of "partial credit-itis." Now he's labeled as unreliable—at best. Incorrect information can be more damaging than correct information can be beneficial.

- Grades aren't everything. Oh, how I wish I understood this sooner. I am walking a very fine line as I write this. On the one hand, I want to support your ambitions, and if your aspirations involve a perfect GPA, then I say, "Go for it!" However, please know that there are things that are more important than your grades. If you allow yourself to become obsessed with your grades, you may lose sight of this. Character, mental health, and happiness are three examples that come to mind. I allowed myself to become so obsessed with my grades as a student that I lost the big picture, and unnecessarily sacrificed my personal and social development on many occasions. Do you know how many times I have been asked about my high school or college GPA outside of an academic setting? Zero. Please understand that this does not mean that I am not encouraging you to do your best. Please, please, please . . . always do your best. However, do not use grades as the sole indicator of your success.

- Sometimes good is good enough. Shooting for straight As in school is admirable. I encourage you to do so. However, shooting for straight As in life is akin to striving for a straitjacket. Life is not about achieving straight As. Attempting to do so will not only drive you nuts, it will reduce your "grade" in the real world because perfection is the enemy of done. You need to learn when to accept a figurative B or C . . . or sometimes even a D or F. In the academic world, the workload will always be manageable by design. The workload will naturally grow without bounds in your life, and only you can decide what is manageable and what is not. Everything can't be a priority to you. You must learn to pick and choose your priorities and let some items fall off your plate.

- Learn from and support your peers. Much of your academic work will be individual assignments and testing. After your formal education, most of your work will likely be group work. Although you will have the occasional group project in school, your grades are ultimately your own. However, learn to embrace and value the role that you play in a team setting. Sometimes you will be the leader, other times you will be a worker bee—be good at both. Additionally, learn to support your peers. Years later, people will not remember your grades, but they will never forget how you treated other people. If you have an opportunity to help your peers, do so. If you have a chance to contribute to someone else's success, do so. Never give in to the temptation to push others down to make yourself look better. Strive to be remembered as kind and helpful first and a good student second.

Learning is a lifelong pursuit, and when approached correctly, your schooling can set the stage for you to be an effective lifelong learner. Fundamentally, this is the number one skill that school can teach you—how to be a lifelong learner. A Chinese proverb states that learning is like rowing upstream; not to advance is to drop back. There is no dropping back when it comes to learning. Never take your foot off the learning gas pedal.

*Love,*

*Dad*

*Dear Hunter*

Let me tell you a story.

Two carpenters, Bill and Bob, break for lunch on a steamy summer day. They rest their bones in the shade and break open their lunch pails. Bill's hands, calloused and covered with sweat-caked sawdust, unwrap his sandwich slowly. He peers underneath a piece of bread to examine its contents.

"DAMMIT!" Bill screams.

"Tuna fish . . . Again!!!  I hate tuna fish!"  His yells slowly reduce to mumbling as he reluctantly bites into the sandwich. "Tuna fish. . . every freaking day. . . if I have to eat tuna fish again, I'm going to fall apart . . . I can't stand it . . . "

Bob was not startled by this outbreak. Bill had been blowing up at lunch every day since he met him five years ago. Bob has resisted the temptation to point out the absurdity of this daily ritual. The enabling silence ends today.

Bob peers into the bottom of an empty Doritos bag and offhandedly remarks, "Hey Bill, I was thinking, maybe you should, uh, you know, let your wife know what type of sandwiches you do like."

Bill responds with a blank stare. "I don't understand."

"I'm just saying, you know, it seems like every day you work yourself up over these sandwiches that you don't like. Maybe it might be worth letting your wife know what type of lunch you would like."

Bill's blank stare breaks only slightly to respond, "Bob, what the hell are you talking about? I make my own lunch."

I know that it may be difficult to imagine someone complaining about lunch that they made for themselves. As I know you can surmise, this humorous anecdote is a metaphor for our lives. We all make our own lunches; however, I cannot tell you how many people I've met that always have something to complain about. Nothing is ever good enough. They are always the victim of some injustice, large or small, that they don't deserve. It seems as if the world is out to get these people. Complaining is exhausting—for the complainer and for everyone around them. Further, it does nothing to solve our problems. Complaining is like rocking in a rocking chair. It gives you something to do, but it gets you nowhere.

Often, these people choose to take their complaints a step further by blaming others for their circumstances. Some people blame their parents, their spouse, their friends, their children, their teacher, their boss, or their co-workers. It seems like these people are oblivious to the fact that if there is someone to blame it is themselves. This is self-sabotaging behavior. Although some people may find solace in taking the burden of their life's situation off of their own shoulders, the reality is that they are undermining their ability to change their circumstances. As soon as we make the decision to blame someone or something else for our issues, we inadvertently give up our own power to change.

In addition to complaining and blaming others, excuse-making completes the ineffectual living trifecta. Some people are full of excuses. I can't do this because of X. I can't do that because of Y. Guess what? X and Y are obstacles that everyone has to deal with. Successful people in life also have to negotiate their way around obstacles. The fact that they are willing to do so makes them successful. In the mind of the excuse maker, they would be successful if it weren't for this and that. If you are so inclined, you can find an excuse to prevent you from doing anything you can think of. You can have excuses or results, but you can't have both.

Complaining, blaming others, and making excuses have one thing in common. They alleviate the necessity for action or change. Therein lies the defense mechanism of these behaviors. Every time you find yourself exhibiting these behaviors remind yourself that this is your lazy self looking for a reason not to take action. If you are ever in need of a challenge, I would encourage you to see how long you can go without complaining, blaming others, or making excuses. Does going one day without any of these behaviors sound easy? Give it a shot—you might be surprised. Even those of us who are not chronically exhibiting this behavior will find this challenge daunting. It wasn't until I embarked on a journey to eliminate these behaviors from my life that I recognized how frequently I was exhibiting them.

Sometimes you might have a reason to complain. Sometimes you might have a reason to blame other people. Sometimes excuses are not really excuses, but instead legitimate reasons. Guess what? There will ALWAYS be a reason to exhibit these behaviors—sound, logical, and reasonable reasons. This is why so many people rely on these behaviors as a crutch; it is so easy to convince ourselves that we really are victims. It is much more difficult to accept responsibility and own the situation. Your character is like a muscle. If you want to strengthen a muscle, you must exert and challenge it. Doing so involves choosing difficult instead of easy. For example, it is difficult to pick up a hundred-pound weight multiple times. It is easy not to. If you want to strengthen your muscles, you will choose the difficult over the easy. The same is true with your character. Choose difficult over easy by resisting the temptation to relieve yourself of responsibility. Making this decision will free you from the chains of inaction and build your character simultaneously.

I recognize this letter may come across as a bit preachy—don't complain, don't blame others, and don't make excuses. Stopping these behaviors is easier said than done. So, what can you do to make this journey of self-restraint easier? Here are some ideas for you that may help.

- Choose optimism—it truly is a choice. Seek out and assume the best in every situation, every place, and every person. There is always a silver lining. Find it. As Noam Chomsky said, "Optimism is a strategy for making a better future. Because unless you believe that the future can be better, it's unlikely you will step up and take responsibility for making it so."

- Embrace the suck. Let's be honest. Sometimes things will truly suck. Yes, find the silver lining. Yes, be optimistic. But the cold hard fact is that every once in a blue moon your situation will flat out suck. In the Navy, we used the term "embrace the suck." This was a tongue-in-cheek coping mechanism that reminded us not to whine, not to complain, and not to try to weasel out of an uncomfortable situation. Instead, we learned to embrace the discomfort. Sometimes you need to learn how to dance in the rain and make the best of a bad decision. Remember that this too shall pass. Complaining and whining won't make a bad situation any better.

- If you must make excuses, follow one rule. Rephrase your excuse. Instead of saying, "I can't make the basketball team because I'm too short," rephrase your excuse to, "I'll have to work extra hard to make the basketball team because I'm shorter than everyone else." The words you choose to use when you communicate matter, especially when you are communicating with yourself.

- Simplify your decision process. When you encounter an undesirable or difficult situation, ask yourself a simple question. "Is there anything that I can do about this?" If the answer is "no," you should be done thinking about it. If the answer is "yes," do it. If you are not willing to take the required action, that's okay too, but make that a deliberate decision that leaves you without worry or regret. I've yet to encounter anything that couldn't be attacked using this process. Is it an oversimplification? Absolutely. However, it can serve to remind us just how simple our response to external events can and should be.

- Beware of the self-serving bias. The self-serving bias is a cognitive bias that explains the tendency for people to take all of the credit for their successes while blaming others for their failures. There will always be people who contribute to your success and others to blame for your failures. Never forget to thank the people who contributed to your success, and never blame anyone for your failures. Failure to do so is a losing life strategy, and unbecoming.

Notwithstanding any of the advice contained in this letter, be gentle with yourself. You are only human. Despite your best efforts you will complain, you will blame others, and you will make excuses from time to time. When you exhibit these behaviors, do your best to acknowledge the negative consequences of this behavior, take a deep breath, and vow to do better in the future.

*Love,*
*Dad*

*Dear Hunter*

You will often hear advice that encourages you to find and pursue your passion. "Do something you love, and you will never work a day in your life" as the saying goes. There is truth to this guidance, but I also want to present you with an alternate way of finding and pursuing your life's passion. For some, the path is clear. I have a friend that dreamed of being a doctor since he was an elementary school student. He pursued his dream on a razor straight path. He is a doctor today and will likely retire as a doctor.

For some, like my doctor friend, their true passion finds them. If you are blessed with a passion that finds you, by all means, you should pursue that passion with every ounce of effort that is in you. However, be careful not to confuse your passion with your current interest. A life's passion is a fire in your belly that cannot be squelched. In fact, it is more than a passion, it is a calling. You think about your calling when you wake up and you dream about it when you sleep. If you are blessed with a calling, you must pursue it. You have no option, and your pursuit is a foregone conclusion. In contrast, a current interest is something that you are very passionate about, but it lacks a certain *je ne sais quoi*. If you are hell-bent on finding your passion or your calling, you can often mistake an interest for a calling.

Why am I splitting hairs between a calling and an interest? Because I was led to believe that we all have a singular purpose in life and it's up to us to find it. As I was frantically searching for my life's purpose, I would sometimes mistake my current interest for a life's calling. This has caused me some confusion and angst over the course of my life. After years of searching and listening to other people's quests, I have come to the conclusion that not everyone has a singular passion or calling that can be categorized uniquely by a type of profession.

For example, although I've had many interests, I never had a burning desire to follow one and only one path in life. I don't think that I am alone in this regard.

Up to this point in my life, I've been on the following "paths" in my life: student, electronics technician, nuclear reactor operator, nuclear engineer, naval submarine officer, military instructor, entrepreneur, radio talk show host, political candidate, power plant operations executive, author, artist, consultant, public speaker, operations consultant, paper manufacturing executive. Many people would look at this life path of sampling and switching careers and professional endeavors and label it as ineffective, confused, or even manic. However, I wouldn't change a thing about my life path choices. I am inclined to sample from the buffet of life rather than indulge in a singular gourmet meal. As a result of this sampling, I have enjoyed a breadth of experiences that would otherwise have been unavailable to me. I believe that this has made me a more well-rounded individual and professional.

I am not encouraging you to follow in my footsteps, but I don't want to dissuade you from doing so either. Conventional wisdom would encourage you to find your path, stick with it, and then climb to the top of that profession and enjoy the gold watch you receive at retirement. Conventional wisdom is conventional for a reason; it tends to work for most people. However, do not feel obligated or pressured to follow this bit of conventional wisdom if your instincts are telling you otherwise. Trust yourself to chart your own path through the wilderness of life. Additionally, I would encourage you to consider the possibility that your life's purpose may not be linked to a professional path. This is a possibility that I've had to come to accept over decades of searching. Maybe your life's purpose is to be a father, or a friend, or a political volunteer. Maybe your life's purpose isn't linked to a specific role. Perhaps your life's purpose is to be a tremendous listener, a problem solver, or a persuasive speaker.

Again, it is possible that you have a calling that is crystal clear to you. If so, congratulations, your search is over. However, if you are like me, the search is a bit more nuanced and the answer may change in various stages of your life. Here are some ideas for identifying and following your life's passion:

- Don't be afraid to follow a general direction, even if you don't know or can't see the specifics. For example, when I was younger I was uncertain what I wanted to do with my life. I knew that I didn't want to work in a cubicle, I wanted to travel, and I wanted to do something with math and science. I discovered an opportunity in the United States Navy to serve aboard nuclear submarines. No one that I knew had ever done such a thing, and even my Navy recruiter had never served on a submarine; therefore, there was nobody to consult to determine what the specifics of serving on a submarine were like. *What was the career trajectory like? What would my day-to-day life be like? What were other submariners like?* However, I sensed that I might like to do something in that general direction, so I took a leap of faith and started down that road. I've learned that life is often like walking in the dark with a flashlight that only allows you to see six inches in front of you. The safest thing to do is to stand still, but we weren't put on this Earth to stand still. Have faith in yourself and trust in the universe to move forward with only six inches of visibility.

- Think about what you have to give to the world. Fulfilling your life's purpose is rarely about satisfying a selfish need. It is my experience that it is more enlightening and revealing when we consider what we have to contribute to the greater good.

We have each been blessed with certain talents and strengths. Consider how to utilize these talents and strengths to make the world a better place—even if it's just improving the lives of your friends, family, or community. Pay attention to the compliments you receive from people. Often these can provide you with clues to your talents and strengths that you may not even realize you have.

- Resist the temptation to follow the money. Money represents options and freedom, and there is certainly nothing wrong with pursuing options and freedom. However, it is my experience that chasing money at the expense of your interests and passions is a losing strategy. There is plenty of money to be made in virtually every career field. Don't be fooled by the averages. Yes, it may be true that a trial attorney makes more than a social psychologist. However, you are not average. Instead consider how the top range of a field does, because if you are passionate about the field, you will certainly find yourself doing better than average.

- Embrace the grind. It is naive to expect that you will always feel passionately invigorated while working towards your professional and personal goals. There will always be elements of any endeavor that are mundane, tiring, and boring. Do not mistake these elements as signs that you are not fulfilling your life's purpose. These mundane elements are known as "the grind." The grind is part of the success of anything worth pursuing and is unavoidable. However, having a passion for the bigger picture is what will carry you through the grind. As Steve Jobs said, "You have to be burning with an idea, or a problem, or a wrong that you want to right. If you're not passionate enough from the start, you'll never stick it out."

- Relax. Your life is special and unique, as are you. There is no "right" way to follow your ambitions and your dreams. Often when we think we are searching for our life's purpose, the reality is that we are training for that purpose. The universe has an uncanny ability to present us our most fulfilling challenges only when we are ready to receive them. There is no such thing as wasted time if you remain open to the possibility that you are being forged in the fire of your own passions. Be patient. Your life is unfolding exactly as it should.

Whether you choose to live your life as I have, like it is a buffet from which to sample, or you have a razor straight line to your life's purpose, enjoy the journey. It is an amazing life, and you have an exciting and promising road ahead of you. Whether you are reading this at the age of 20 or 70, the best is yet to come. Remain open and curious throughout your life's journey, and you will land exactly where you were intended to land.

*Love,*
*Dad*

*Dear Hunter*

Life is beautiful. Our world is full of opportunities to live, love, and laugh. If I made a list of all the things that I was grateful for, I suspect it would be longer than the length of this book. However, there are no highs without some lows, and there are some very low lows. In fact, you will have days that just suck. Even the most optimistic and enlightened among us have days that challenge their Zen-like life perspective. When you have these days, there's not much that anyone can say that can make you feel better, but I'm your father, so I am going to try.

I'd like to share with you an example of a bad day in my life. I was a sophomore in high school. The school was holding a pep rally assembly before the opening day of the football season. I was a proud member of the varsity football team—maybe too proud. I felt pretty damn cool wearing my football jersey to school that day. The entire school was assembled in the gymnasium to show their support to the football team. The band played and the cheerleaders cheered. The energy in the gymnasium was palpable. I was seated in the bleachers with the rest of the football team. I looked into the crowds. I saw my non-football playing friends in the sophomore class section and my girlfriend in the junior class section. I was beaming with pride to be a football player that day. The head football coach took center stage with a microphone and was pumping up the student body as he talked about the upcoming game against our rival team, Pompton Lakes. Then he called out to the football team to join him on the gym floor. The crowd cheered. The team leapt off the bleachers.

Let me explain something to you before I continue the story. The bleachers that we were sitting on were the old-style bleachers that expand out from the gym wall. When they are pulled out, they need to be locked into a place to prevent them from retracting back into the wall. Well, whoever pulled out the bleachers that day didn't lock them. So, any sudden force inward causes the bleachers to rapidly retract. Any sudden force? Do I mean like 30 football players leaping off the bleaches at the same time? Yes.

I was seated on the top row of the bleachers, and as I tried to join my team, the bleachers rapidly slammed shut. I tried to leap off the top row, but my leg got caught in the bleacher. I toppled forward headfirst towards the ground. Of course, I didn't land on the ground but instead was suspended from the top row of the bleachers by my right ankle. I was dangling from the bleachers with my back towards the entire student body with my football jersey prominently displaying my last name, DiGeronimo, so as to leave no doubt in any of the students' minds who I was. The football team was circled around the head coach hooting and hollering and were oblivious to my fate. I was stuck mid-air for less than a minute before the high school baseball coach rushed to my rescue, but it felt like an eternity. I picked up a nickname from this event . . . "bleacher creature," which stuck for the better part of my high school career. Needless to say, I was beyond embarrassed. I was mortified. *How could I ever walk down the hallways of the high school again? How could I face my girlfriend? Was she embarrassed too?*

Like most embarrassing moments, it wasn't as bad as I imagined. Life went on, as it always does. Did people, including my friends, have a healthy laugh at my expense? Absolutely. Is that the worst thing in the world? Of course not. I had built up the consequences in my head to an irrational level. When we are embarrassed, especially if we are prone to self-consciousness, we become very self-focused in light of an embarrassing event. So much so that we experience "empathy neglect." Empathy neglect causes one to fail to consider the substantial amount of empathy that people feel for someone in an embarrassing situation. Think about how you feel when something embarrassing happens to someone else. Are you more likely to judge the person and think they are an idiot, or cringe on their behalf because you feel bad for them? People are generally empathetic, so don't assume the worst. Pick yourself up, dust yourself off, laugh at yourself, and move on down the road.

I should make something clear, getting stuck in the bleachers as a young high schooler in front of all of my friends and peers was deeply embarrassing, but it certainly wasn't tragic. This letter is not about dealing with tragic events. Death, destruction, illness, and terror are topics unto themselves, and I am not addressing those in this letter. I guess you could call my embarrassing day a "first world problem," as many of our problems tend to be. But that plays well into my first piece of advice regarding dealing with an embarrassing moment or an otherwise bad day. Remind yourself that this is not a life-or-death circumstance. Be grateful that it wasn't and know that someday you will be able to laugh about it.

Singular moments such as this one can make an otherwise average day feel like a horrible day. But what about days when nothing seems to go your way? You wake up late. You spill your coffee on your dress shirt. You hit unexpected traffic making you even later. Your boss spots you arriving late and calls you out on it. Your presentation bombs. Your favorite team loses. You lose your phone. Ughh. . . *Could this day get any worse?!?!* What then?

When all else seems to fail, breathe. Just breathe. Focus on your breath. I know what you are thinking . . .*That's not going to help.* Yes, it will. Inhale for six seconds and exhale for four seconds. Repeat ten times. As you do this, drown out your surroundings and try to clear your mind. As thoughts come racing through your mind, as they inevitably will, observe them as if you are standing by the side of the highway and your thoughts are the cars racing by. Watch them come and go without judgement. Inhale for six seconds and exhale for four seconds.

After you breathe, remind yourself that life will never be perfect. As Leo Tolstoy said, "If you look for perfection, you'll never be content." Life is beautiful, but it can also be messy. If you want to avoid days like these entirely, stay in bed for the rest of your life. Don't do anything. Don't go anywhere. Don't say anything. Otherwise, days like this are part of the deal. Think about your best days. Think about the days when everything went well, and you were basking in the thrill of life. Remind yourself that there will be more of those days in your future. Today is the price we pay for those wonderful days.

Also, avoid speaking in absolutes when things aren't going your way. For example, *This always happens to me! I never do anything right.* Words matter. Don't allow yourself to be a victim of circumstances. This doesn't always happen to you, but it is happening now. As soon as you give yourself permission to be a victim the universe has a strange way of proving you right, which is the last thing that you need today. Even on the worst day, you can usually identify some things that you should and can do differently in the future to prevent this from happening again. Doing so restores your power and eliminates the temptation to make yourself a victim.

You may not be able to change what has happened to you today, but you can certainly change the way you respond to it. I have found humor to be one of the more powerful responses to a day when things just aren't going your way. Sometimes all you can and should do is laugh. John Lennon may have lamented that "nobody told me that there'd be days like this," but you will have a different story. I, your father, am telling you that there will be days like this, and I am asking you to take it in stride, accept your circumstances with dignity and grace, and enjoy a good laugh at your own expense.

*Love,*
*Dad*

*Dear Hunter*

Blaise Pascal said, "All of humanity's problems stem from man's inability to sit quietly in a room alone." Try it. Sit quietly alone with no distractions: computers, phones, books, etc. I'm not talking about meditation or a mindfulness exercise. Just set a timer for five minutes and sit in a chair doing nothing. If you are like me, after a few minutes you start to fidget for something to do. Five minutes?! The purpose of this exercise is to show you just how hard doing "nothing" can be.

How often do you consider "nothing" as the ideal action? When you think about doing "nothing" what associations come to mind? Lazy, unsuccessful, stagnant? Of course you do! We are programmed to act, to make, to create, to decide, to lead, to manage, to plan, to evaluate, to analyze, to teach, to mentor, to perform, to contribute, to support, to consult . . . To do nothing? Where is that on the list? We are hardwired for action. However, sometimes nothing is precisely the right thing to do. Keep that in mind as an option when you are contemplating a decision. It has been said that intelligence is knowing what to say and wisdom is knowing whether to say it. Just because you are faced with a stimulus does not mean that you have to have a reaction. Learn to be deliberate about your words and actions.

Admittedly, sometimes inaction is not a deliberate decision. Sometimes, if not often, inaction is reflective of the paralysis that stems from the "freeze" in the fight, flight, or freeze response to a threatening stimulus. However, it is the connotation of "nothing" being the choice of the cowardly and the fearful that gives the option a bad name. The Hippocratic Oath is "First do no harm" for a reason. It is better for a doctor to do nothing than to harm a patient. Intellectually, we can acknowledge the benefits of the Hippocratic Oath. Unfortunately, few of us have the emotional strength to admit that our best and most well-intended efforts can often make a situation worse. The reason that this is often the case is that there are always unintended consequences to our actions. Always. It is prudent to think these consequences through before inadvertently making a situation worse.

In 2005, a Los Angeles class fast-attack nuclear submarine, the USS San Francisco (SSN-711), was cruising submerged at nearly top speed when it crashed into an underwater sea mountain. Everyone aboard was thrown violently about the submarine. There were many injured sailors. Sadly, one sailor did not survive his injuries. The damage to the submarine, as you might expect, was extensive. The consequences of this incident rippled throughout the entire nuclear submarine community. I'm not going to delve into the details of why the collision occurred, but suffice to say, a formal investigation revealed that the nuclear submarine community had to improve upon its basic navigational skill sets. As a result, the leaders of the submarine community instituted new requirements of training and qualification for all matters related to navigation. Reasonable people could, and did, disagree with this decision. The United States Navy has been operating submarines for decades and this was the first time a collision of this nature occurred. However, those in charge couldn't possibly conclude that we didn't need to do anything. *We must do something, right? Something is better than nothing, right?* At the risk of sounding like I am disagreeing with the decisions of the United States Navy, I would contend the answer is "maybe." Something is not necessarily better than nothing, but it might be. However, first do no harm, and second, consider the unintended consequences.

In this particular instance, I did not see that these additional requirements would cause harm. However, they did have unintended consequences that I did not believe were thought through. Specifically, these extra requirements would mean that something else would be neglected. There is no standing around looking for something to do in the world of nuclear submarines. In fact, I've never worked in an environment with a more demanding, jam-packed schedule than on a nuclear submarine. From 0600 to 1800, at a minimum, the schedule had virtually no white space. I remember thinking, *These new requirements are great, in theory, but something is going to fall off the plate by adding new requirements.* What would fall off the plate? Since there was no deliberate plan to have these new training and qualification requirements replace x, y, and z, the consequences were unknown. Are we creating a giant game of whack-a-mole? Specifically, we improve in the area of navigation but fall back in another area? In the Navy, we would say that you can fit only five pounds of "stuff" in a five-pound bag. Unfortunately, we were routinely asked to fit ten pounds of "stuff" in a five-pound bag and left to our own devices to determine which five pounds would be left out of the bag.

I share this story with you not because I want to disparage the Navy's decision making; however, I want to make you aware that we often do this in our lives. Something sudden happens and we vow to add a "requirement" to our life. Maybe you decide that you want to start spending an hour a day at the gym. We add more and more and more requirements to our daily life and then we wonder why we are stressed and overwhelmed. I would encourage you to consider removing something from your life every time you add something new. This can even apply to your material possessions; if you buy a new shirt, commit to donating an older shirt to charity. If you don't, you will ultimately find your life "cluttered" both literally, with material possessions, and figuratively, with demands on your time.

In a similar way, sometimes removing things from our life is all that we need to improve our current situation. Using the example that I gave about the Navy, maybe the existing navigation training and qualification were adequate but were viewed as "stuff" that didn't make the cut to fit into the five-pound sack. Maybe, the Navy could have considered what requirements could be removed from the life of their submariners so that the requirements remaining would get the attention that they deserved. It is rumored that the Renaissance artist Michelangelo was once asked about the challenges he faced while sculpting his masterpiece *David*. Legend has it that his response was, "It is easy. You just chip away the stone that doesn't look like David." Similarly, sometimes in life you need to remove anything that doesn't support your vision for your future. Easy? Hell, no. If it were easy everyone would have the life of their dreams. What's easy is saying *yes* to everything that comes across your plate. As a result, you end up with a very cluttered life and mind. Focusing on what really matters to you, or creating the sculpture of your dreams, requires chipping away at anything that doesn't support your priorities.

A similar thought process can be said for the spoken and written word. There is a story about Winston Churchill that has stuck with me. The story goes that his staff brought him a report on a particular topic for him to review. Churchill looked at the size of the report and said, "Nope. It's too long. Make it shorter." His staff took the report back to the drawing board and removed all of the unnecessary information. They brought the report back to Churchill. He leafed through the report, looked at his staff and said, "Nope. Still too long." His staff, exasperated, repeated the process of paring the report down to its nuts and bolts. When they handed Churchill the report for the third time, he once again told them that the report was too long. At their wit's end, a member of his staff said, "Sir. We can't make this report any shorter. We have boiled it down to its bare essentials." To which, Churchill responded, "Perfect. Thank you" and took the report. This story highlights the fact that in both the written and spoken word it is easy to drone on and on, but it takes real effort to distill your thoughts. In fact, I have found the power of one's words increases as the volume of one's words decreases.

On that note, as Mark Twain said, "I apologize for such a long letter – I didn't have time to write a short one."

*Love,*
*Dad*

*Dear Hunter*

Sigh. Here we go. I could not omit the topic of politics, even though it is a minefield through which I am reluctant to tread. I hope that the political landscape is less treacherous as you are reading this than it is as I am writing this letter. Other than religion, there is perhaps no more emotionally charged topic than politics. This has been true for thousands of years and will likely be true for thousands more. My objective in this letter is to discuss how to best handle and think about politics, without disclosing my own political perspectives.

On one hand, I encourage you to be an informed and active citizen because, as a society, how we govern is reflective of our collective values. Our values shape our character and I encourage you to participate in the creation and protection of our national character. However, on the other hand, politics are messy. There may be no quicker way to lose your innocence than by taking a jaunt into the political arena. I learned this the hard way.

In 2012, I had recently retired from the United States Navy and was running a mergers & acquisitions company in Honolulu Hawaii. Long story made short, I decided to run for U.S. Congress for the 2nd congressional district in the state of Hawaii. I lost in the primary election. Longer story made short; I then became a talk show host on a radio program that primarily covered political topics. These two life experiences taught me a lot about how to navigate politics and the political arena that I would like to share with you.

The first thing that you should recognize about politics is that it has become the country's most elaborate soap opera. There are good guys and bad guys, plots and subplots, twists and turns, and cliff-hangers. However, unlike a soap opera, we don't all agree on who the good guys and bad guys are. In fact, we tend to be split, nearly down the middle, in our assessment of who is "good" and who is "bad." George Washington, in his farewell address, warned the nation to beware of the spirit of the political party. I tend to agree. I have observed that people tend to formulate their opinions about what is right and wrong along political party lines instead of fundamental principles. This has always confused me. The more I have thought about it, the more I have to believe that this phenomenon is a result of an evolutionary characteristic—specifically, the need to stick with our "tribe" for security.

Consider something as innocuous as watching a football game. The first question someone who enters the room asks is, "Who are you rooting for?" Similarly, if you are in the middle of watching a movie and someone joins mid-movie, you can bet they will ask, "Is he a good guy or a bad guy?" We align ourselves with groups in all that we do, so why should politics be any different? Unfortunately, this makes having a constructive conversation about public policy very challenging. If the "good guy" says "X" and the "bad guy" says "Y," more often than not people will defend "X" without taking the time to consider the possibility that "Y" may be more correct.

What makes the defense of "X" versus "Y" even more absurd, in my estimation, is that generally, all political parties desire a result of a policy that is similar, but differ in their opinions on how to get there. I've yet to hear a politician say that they want poor healthcare, substandard education, less secure national security, or inequitable social justice. The differences that exist between political parties are generally not in the desired outcomes, but in the proposed paths. Therefore, if we could eliminate the emotion associated with viewing politics from a" good guys" versus "bad guys" lens, our conversations would be focused on the virtues of various methods to achieve our nation's goals.

My recommendation to you when discussing politics is to focus on the desired result. Take an example such as income inequality, which is clearly an issue that needs to be addressed in our country because the gap between the wealthy and the poor is growing at an alarming rate. Instead of launching into a heated debate about why we need to do x, y, and z to address income inequality, ask two questions first. The first question is: Do you believe that income inequality is an issue that needs to be addressed in our country? The second question is: Do you believe that the role of the federal government includes addressing this issue? My opinion is that these are the basic questions that need to be answered before delving into details about x, y, and z.

The second question in particular is one that I would encourage you to think long and hard about when it comes to addressing problems in our country. I have observed folks who automatically assume that all problems should be addressed by the federal government. At the risk of exposing my political leanings, as I said I wanted to avoid, I would contend that the federal government is not always the conduit to solve our problems. In fact, you could make a reasonable case that sometimes the government has made our problems worse. Rarely, in my opinion, do our elected officials choose to make our problems worse, but there are always unintended consequences to all actions of the government. Sometimes, these unintended consequences need to be identified, addressed, and rectified. For example, you could easily make the case that our system of government has exacerbated the income gap by allowing, and encouraging, lobbyists to influence politicians, resulting in preferred treatment for groups that can afford lobbyists.

Another item worth discussing is the motivation of our elected officials. You have to ask yourself, why is the federal government not better about solving problems? When you consider that most of our nation's problems have remained the same for at least my lifetime, you have to believe that either these problems are unsolvable or maybe our elected officials are not particularly adept at problem-solving. There is a truly cynical perspective, which I choose not to subscribe to, that politicians don't solve problems because they rely on these problems to be elected. That, if true, would be a very depressing and large pill to swallow. While I do not assign such malintent to our politicians, I do have to conclude that problem solving is not their number one priority. Let's face it—their number one priority is getting re-elected. What is the key to being re-elected? Sadly, it is money. Did you know that in all federal elections in the past 40 years, the candidate with the larger political coffers won over 90 percent of the time? So, if fundraising is a politician's number one priority, it is easier to understand why we don't see more problems solved. The reality is that most of the financial resources that are available to politicians come from sources that are doing fairly well in the current system—if they weren't, they wouldn't have the money to donate. If a politician relies on these funds to be re-elected, and these funds generally come from people who are content with the status quo, is it any surprise that true reform rarely originates from the halls of government?

Be wary of political discussions with friends and family. I have never witnessed a political debate that ended with one party saying, "You know what? You are right and I am wrong. Thank you for showing me the error of my ways." Don't get into the habit of trying to convince people to change their political viewpoint. There is rarely a "right" or "wrong" point of view, regardless of how certain you are about your own vantage point. Related, always remain open to the possibility that your views will change with time. That is normal. Resist the temptation to clutch your political views so tightly that you lose the ability to calmly and rationally consider other viewpoints. Don't fall into the trap that Mark Twain commented on when he said,

"It is easier to fool people than it is to convince them that they have been fooled."

With all that being said, I encourage you to be an informed citizen and a participant in the democratic process in the manner that you see fit. Taking action, directly or indirectly, to contribute towards a greater country and a brighter future is always a valiant endeavor. As Winston Churchill said, "'Many forms of Government have been tried, and will be tried in this world of sin and woe. No one pretends that democracy is perfect or all-wise. Indeed it has been said that democracy is the worst form of Government except for all those other forms that have been tried from time to time."

*Love,*
*Dad*

*Dear Hunter*

I am deviating a bit from the general theme of these letters by sharing some thoughts with you about the almighty dollar. I would never encourage you to pursue riches for riches sake. However, make no mistake; money can provide you with options and freedom. Be careful though, as the pursuit of money can actually take away options and freedom from you. Many people spend their lifetimes chasing the dollar, giving away their options and freedom today for a chance at wealth tomorrow. There is a virtue in making sacrifices today for a payoff tomorrow, but this must be done thoughtfully and in moderation. It is my experience that most wealth or financial freedom is built through the creation of and adherence to disciplined habits combined with a fundamental understanding of some financial basics.

The most powerful and impactful piece of advice that I can offer you regarding your personal finances is also the simplest. Save ten percent of every dollar that you make. It is so important that I'll repeat it—save ten percent of every dollar that you make. This is your rainy-day money and your retirement money. Do NOT wait until you are making a better salary, or you are married, or you buy your first house, etc. Implement this savings plan with your very first job by investing in a broad-based index fund such as the SP500.

Albert Einstein famously said, "Compound interest is the 8th wonder of the world. He who understands it, earns it. He who doesn't, pays it." Let's take a look at what he meant. Let's say that you save $2500 a year starting when you are 18 and continue doing that until you are 30. Assuming an annual return of 9 percent, this savings will be worth $1.2 million dollars when you are 65. Let's compare this to a scenario where you wait until you are 30 and save $2500 a year every year until you are 65. In the first case you are saving money for 12 years and in the second case you are saving money for 35 years.

Using the same assumptions, your nest egg when you wait until you are 30 to start saving would be worth $590,000. This is half the amount that you would have saved had you started at the age of 18. Albert Einstein was known as a pretty smart guy for a reason.

The sad truth is that almost every person that I know was taught some version of this example at a very young age. However, very few people execute this strategy because it is so easy to convince themselves that they will start saving next month or next year. Months slip into years and years into decades in the blink of an eye. That is why so many people end up panicking as they get older for fear that they will have to work for the rest of their lives because they cannot afford to retire. Please don't fall into this trap. Save ten percent of everything that you make and put it somewhere that you don't have convenient access to. There are very few pieces of advice in this book that I would consider "direct orders" from father to son. This is one of them. I'll say it again, save ten percent of everything you earn.

The second most powerful piece of financial advice that I can give you is to avoid debt. Debt can be a crippling weight on your shoulders if you aren't careful. Unfortunately, debt creeps into our lives, and its weight is felt only incrementally over time. The people I know who have become suffocated with debt didn't create their problem overnight. The best way to avoid creating a long-term debt problem for yourself is to steer clear of the use of credit cards until you can use them simply as a convenience. More specifically, only use credit cards when you can pay off the balance monthly. If you are holding balances on a credit card, consider this a red flag that you are headed into financial danger.

Additionally, I encourage, implore, and demand that you develop a habit of living below your means. I can't even begin to explain the emotional duress that you will avoid by doing so. The stress associated with living paycheck to paycheck or living in fear that you will lose your job because you can't afford to be jobless is unspeakably painful. One of the simplest ways to live below your means is to avoid the temptation to upgrade your standard of living when you receive a raise. It is a natural tendency to want to buy a new car, rent a nicer apartment, or buy a bigger home every time you feel like you can now afford to do so. It's a trap! Don't do it. Learn to be comfortable living beneath your means. The same is true with possessions. Less is more. I remember when I first started making money, I was always buying things that made me feel better about myself. They were not outlandishly extravagant items, but they were unnecessary. I was a sucker for books, music, and art. What I found over time is that they only made me feel good for a short period of time. The high associated with buying new things wore off quickly while I was left being weighed down with possessions I didn't need or want. Living a lean life is refreshing and liberating. I would encourage you to embrace a minimalist lifestyle as it relates to possessions. As Tyler Durden said in the movie *Fight Club*, "The things you own, end up owning you."

Minimizing your possessions has the advantage of allowing you to save more money. However, there is a difference between being frugal and stingy. I encourage you to be frugal and warn you against being stingy. Being stingy is not only an unbecoming trait, but it is also, in my opinion, unhealthy because it is based on fear. Specifically, stingy people are fearful about their futures and have a scarcity mindset. Conversely, you can, and should, be frugal while maintaining a healthy sense of security in your future and a mindset of abundance. Finding the line between frugality and stinginess can be challenging. One of the elements of doing so requires you to place a value on your time. For example, let's say you are buying a new television. There is a store five minutes from your home that sells the television that you want for $300. There is another store that is an hour away that sells the television for $290. Would you travel the extra two hours (one hour in each direction) to save ten dollars? If not, that means you value your time at more than five dollars an hour. There is, however, some dollar value of savings for which you would travel the extra two hours. You should know that value and re-evaluate it periodically. Knowing this value will assist you in determining whether you will pay to have your lawn cut, your sidewalk shoveled, your oil changed, or whether you will do these things yourself. Having a time value of money allows you to make financial decisions with a true north to guide you.

I would be remiss not to mention charity when discussing your finances. I encourage you to foster a charitable spirit. This can mean different things to different people. For some, it means donating money to charity, and to others, it means helping family, friends, or even strangers who are in need. Personally, I prefer to look for opportunities to help other people individually, rather than donating money to charity. Admittedly, I am somewhat suspicious of charities because I can't see where my money is going. Perhaps that's too cynical of me, but that's how I feel. However, I do and encourage you to help when you can. For example, if I am walking down the street and someone asks me for money, most of the time if I have cash on me, I give it away. I have been teased for this tendency. *Don't you know that they are just going to buy drugs with that?* Well, actually, I don't know that. I sometimes think that most of us are a few mistakes away from needing help ourselves. If I can help, I will. Have I been burned because of this attitude? Absolutely. However, I would rather be able to help one person that is truly in need even if it means being burned nine other times. I encourage you to embrace a similar philosophy. One of the most human gestures we can make is to help other humans in need. Additionally, the universe has a well-deserved reputation for rewarding charitable acts many times over.

*Love,*
*Dad*

*Dear Hunter*

You are watching a baseball game. The centerfielder dives for a fly ball. The ball skips off the ground and into his glove. However, as he gets up, he holds the ball in his glove towards the umpire in an attempt to signal that he caught the ball before it hit the ground. He knows he didn't. Is the baseball player lacking integrity?

Your best friend tells you that he is planning to propose marriage to his girlfriend. For a variety of reasons, you think that he is making a mistake. However, you congratulate him and tell him how happy you are for him. Are you lacking integrity?

The general manager of a power plant is preparing his revenue forecast for next years' budget. His boss encourages him to overstate his projections. The general manager believes that the company is being considered for acquisition, and he is being asked to inflate the numbers to increase the value of the company. He acquiesces and inflates the numbers. Is the general manager lacking integrity?

I lead with these scenarios because all too often discussions about integrity present the topic as black and white, and I would contend that real-world scenarios are rarely black and white. Before proceeding, let's define *integrity*. What is integrity? The definition that has served me well is this: "Integrity is doing the right thing, even when no one is watching." Should integrity be a core value and guiding principle for the decisions that you make in life? Absolutely—without a doubt!  However, often acting with integrity is black and white only insofar as what is "right" is black and white. Life can be messy. Sometimes you will find that it is challenging to determine what is "right." Other times you will find that the "right" thing is obvious but following through with the necessary action is not so easy.

By introducing the topic with the "gray" nature of integrity, I risk sending you the wrong message. Specifically, I hope that your entering argument into any situation is that you are committed to doing the right thing. I have observed that people who look for the "gray" nature of right and wrong are more inclined to travel down a slippery slope that rarely leads to a good place. So, what are the virtues of living a life of integrity? Without delving too deeply into the pool of theology, I'd be remiss not to include a brief discussion about our responsibilities as humans. All major world religions include a "code of conduct" that is professed to be the expectations of our maker. I don't think it is a coincidence that all of these codes of conduct explicitly state the expectation of being a virtuous human being. Theology is something that you will have to come to terms with on your own. However, although I won't claim to have a full grasp on why we are on this Earth (I'm still working on figuring that out), I do believe with all of my heart that a component of our mission in this life is to be kind, compassionate, and considerate of others. Living a life of integrity is central to our ability to do so. If you don't believe me, could you imagine routinely doing the "wrong" thing because you felt like it? How would this make people in your life feel? As importantly, how would you feel? The standard of integrity is forged into our soul at birth. Deviations from this can, and will, weigh heavily on your heart.

Why do we feel this weight? I believe it is because our soul yearns for harmony. We are at peace when we become the person that our soul wants us to be. When we are not fully self-integrated, meaning that there is a disconnect between who we want to be and who we are, we become riddled with inner conflict and guilt. The longer we live with this disharmonious mismatch, the wider the gap between our idealized self and our actual self becomes. The wider the gap, the more difficult bridging the gap becomes. Sadly, for some people, the gap becomes so wide that they just learn to live with it, but the gap's existence prevents people from feeling at peace with themselves and the world. Moral of the story: Actively work to keep the gap between who you want to be and who you are as small as possible. Perfection may be unattainable, but the inner peace that comes from trying your best is worth the effort.

It has been said that you should live your life as if the walls can talk because eventually, they will. Try as one might, eventually your reputation will be the one that you earned and the one that you deserve. There really are no off-camera moments. The truth has a way of coming out. You can't always make everyone happy, and you will undoubtedly disappoint people from time to time, but I encourage you to live in such a way that when the truth comes out, as it always does, people will know that you are a man of principle and a man of integrity.

An example from my life comes to mind. I was running a mergers & acquisitions company in Honolulu, Hawaii. My company assisted business owners in the sale of their businesses. Selling small to medium-sized businesses is challenging beyond description primarily because things are often not as they appear. Some, but not all, of the business owners that I dealt with had an uncanny ability to make their businesses appear more profitable than they actually were. This created a unique challenge for my company because our clients were the business owners and the more the businesses sold for, the more money we made. There were times when it would have been convenient and profitable to look the other way. However, this was not consistent with my own internal moral compass. For example, we had one client that owned a seemingly successful construction company. During our due diligence, everything checked out—tax returns, profit and loss statements, receipts, invoices, and bank statements. Further, the business owners had great reputations as pillars of the community. However, something didn't feel right to me. I didn't know what it was, but something was amiss and my "spidey senses" were tingling. Without any specific evidence to substantiate my concerns, and with payroll to make and bills to pay, we proceeded with representing this client. Fast forward to the closing procedure with the buyers. They were well-financed and experienced but clearly, they were not familiar with how to evaluate and analyze a business sale. They were jumping without looking into a several-million-dollar investment. I was very uneasy. I still had a sense that something was wrong with the business. However, it was not my company's responsibility to unearth every rock to prove it. After all, we represented them. The buyers, however, typically employ a team of accountants and attorneys in an attempt to validate the financial and operational records provided by the seller. The buyer's team conducted a cursory review of the records. We were nearing completion of the review process where the final documents completing the sale would be signed. I was uncomfortable and anxious. *What should I do? Do I turn a blind eye and allow my company to collect its fee and move on with life?*

I decided to discuss the situation with my staff. They all stood to earn a nice payout if the sale went through. However, I respected their opinions and thought they might agree that we should do something other than blindly allow the sale to proceed. In fact, they were without exception flat out mad at me. *We represent the seller. We did our due diligence, and everything checked out. Who are we to tell the buyer that they haven't evaluated the business closely enough?!* They had a point, but my inner self was telling me otherwise. After a sleepless night, I made a tough decision. I drafted a letter from me to the buyers stating that it was my professional opinion that their review of the business and its records was cursory and inadequate. I stated that although I was not blocking the sale of the business, I wanted to document my concerns. This highly unusual act had several consequences. For starters, it spooked the buyers and delayed the closing. My staff was furious with me and my client threatened to take legal action against me if the deal fell through. Admittedly, I was doubting my decision. It would have been so easy, and convenient, to keep my mouth shut. But I just couldn't; my moral compass wouldn't let me.

To make a long story short, our client was, in fact, cooking the books. Their business was fraudulent, and they had been misrepresenting their financial performance and health. There was no way my company could have uncovered this because the documents they provided us were clean. However, eventually, the buyers' accountants and attorneys uncovered the truth. The sale did not go through, and the buyers dodged a bullet that would have cost them their life savings.

Integrity has been described as the willingness to do what is right over what is convenient. You will be amazed how often an opportunity to take a shortcut around integrity will present itself to you. I swear it feels like the universe is intent on tempting us, especially when we are at our weakest. Unless you have prepared yourself for this eventuality, the temptation to take the path of least resistance may be too great for you to withstand. Plant the seed in your brain, right now, that when faced with an option of doing what is right versus what is convenient, you will choose right. It often takes every ounce of strength and integrity you have to persevere and choose right over convenience. Every time you choose right, you are investing in yourself and in your future.

I cannot tell you that I have always followed my moral compass. But I can tell you that the times when I haven't represent the largest regrets of my life. The weight of these regrets is heavy. I wish for you to avoid the life sentence of having to carry this weight. Live a life of integrity, my son, the universe will reward you and your soul will thank you.

*Love,*
*Dad*

*Dear Hunter*

I grew up with sports—baseball, basketball, and football to be specific. Sports are what I thought about when I woke up, what I played in all of my free time, what I spent my money on (collector cards, magazines, etc.), what I talked about with my parents and friends, what I thought about before I went to sleep, and what I dreamed about. Sounds like sports was my first love—I guess it was. Although my interests diversified as I got older, sports remained the central interest of my life until I graduated high school.

After high school graduation, I played the occasional intramural league, but for the most part my love affair with sports ended abruptly. This included my interest in watching and following professional sports. Not unlike a heartbroken lover, I couldn't stand to watch the former love of my life live on without me. I felt betrayed. Melodramatic? I suppose, but it's how I felt. It wasn't until many years later that I returned to sports as a spectator and fan. Although in retrospect I should have realized my dreams of becoming a professional athlete were not realistic, this was the first and strongest dream of my life. Giving up this dream wasn't easy, but eventually I had to let it go.

When I think about all that I sacrificed for sports, I sometimes question if my time devoted to sports was wasted time. Would I have been better off learning musical instruments, playing life sports like tennis and golf, devoting more time to academics or volunteer opportunities? Did I limit expanding my horizons? Would I be a better person today if I had spent my youth on more diversified or noble endeavors? These are questions that I have wrestled with my entire adult life. I had made peace with myself by accepting the fact that the past is gone and lamenting it is a fruitless endeavor; however, now that you are in my life, these questions have surfaced again.

Although the decision to participate in organized sports is ultimately yours, as your father, I feel like I have the ability to influence that decision to a certain extent.

I think back to my childhood and I reflect quite fondly on the time spent with my father playing sports together. I remember weekends spent playing catch, taking batting practice, fielding ground balls, shooting hoops, or tossing around the football. My father's enthusiasm for sports was infectious. Sports were our bond. Whether it was playing, watching, or talking, sports was the conduit through which my father taught me his philosophies of life. Sports were our common ground that we could always walk on together, regardless of what stage of life we were in. No matter what, we always had sports to fall back on.

I really did enjoy playing sports. There was no undue pressure from my father, but there was an expectation, which I gladly and willingly upheld. Despite the heartbreak that I ultimately experienced after my high school sports career ended, I am thankful for my sports experiences because they substantially contributed to the person that I have become. Do I know how to play the piano or violin? No, but there are substantial benefits that I reaped from my experiences as an athlete. (Although I will elaborate on those benefits, I think it is important to note that not all childhood endeavors must result in long-term benefits. There is something to be said for joy for the sake of joy.)

The first benefit of a childhood devoted to team sports is developing confidence. Times may have changed, but when I was growing up, the number one way to make friends was through sports. Sports was the language and currency of my peers. If I reflect on every friend that I have from my youth, many of whom I remain friends with today, I can trace the origins of our friendship back to sports—some from organized sports, some from sports played in the neighborhood streets, and some from a shared love of the sport. I know there are other ways to make friends, and I suspect that if I had had other interests, I'd have made friends through those interests. However, there was a confidence that I developed from excelling in sports that I don't think could have been replaced with other interests. This confidence was reflected in my ability to interact with other people my age but also, in a more lasting sense, sports gave me the confidence to try new things and put myself out there.

I remember being fearful and reluctant to step up to the plate as a 2nd grader to face the league's fastest pitcher, but the pressure of being part of a team forced me to face my fears. I clearly recall getting a base hit off this same pitcher and feeling like I had just conquered the world. Being exposed to challenges that seemed insurmountable and then rising to the occasion was a common occurrence in my athletic career. This has directly contributed to my ability and willingness to face challenges in my life. Sports are an effective way of allowing us to grow comfortable with feeling uncomfortable and doing our job despite our fear.

Another benefit of sports is that they force continuous personal development and improvement. No matter how talented you are, no matter how good you become, there is always someone better. There is always a team out there who is ready to beat you soundly. Although, in life, your principal opponent is the man in the mirror, sports force you to find the strength and courage to push the man in the mirror to levels of performance that might not be possible without the spirit of competition. There is an element of competition that ignites a flame inside of us that can remain extinguished in the absence of competition. It is this inner flame that can push you to wake up at 5 a.m. to lift weights in the gym or practice your free-throw shots. It is this inner flame that can keep you running wind sprints in basketball practice when every ounce of your body is screaming for you to stop. I have found that direct competition fades away as you move away from sports, but there is always some sense of competition that remains. In the Navy and in the business world, my willingness to not shy away from competition, especially against a person or team that appears to be more talented, stems directly from my background in sports.

Teamwork is king and the team always comes before each individual player. There is no substitute for team sports when it comes to learning these lessons. The most painful but lasting lesson in teamwork occurred when I was a sophomore in high school. In baseball, I had always been our team's shortstop. Starting in 2nd grade: on every little league team, every all-star team, every summer league team, and our freshman baseball team, I was the shortstop. That was my position and I assumed it always would be. Sophomore year that changed abruptly, which was a painful experience for me that impacted my self-identity. As it turned out, there wasn't a junior or senior class player on the baseball team who was competitive for the shortstop position that year. During the summer between freshman and sophomore year, I had played with the varsity players as the shortstop and had a great season. The varsity shortstop position was mine to lose, and I lost it. There was another player in the sophomore class who had developed to be a much better hitter than I was. On the field defensively, we were probably similar, but I certainly didn't do myself any favors in pre-season in that area. Not only was I weak at the plate; I was a mess in the field. I made errors that were uncharacteristic of me and then I got into my own head and my performance went downhill from there. The coach made the decision to put my peer in as shortstop one day during practice and he never looked back. That player, Sal, remained our shortstop for our high school career. I did make the varsity team that sophomore year as a backup outfielder and pitcher, but I spent the majority of the season on the bench watching "my position" played by someone else. Although I was hurt deeply inside, the truth was that the coach made the right decision. I could have been bitter, I could have quit the team, I could have complained, but I did my best to put on a happy face. Team before individual, even when it hurts.

The last life lesson that I will highlight about sports is that they gave me the courage to be "in the arena." Theodore Roosevelt delivered a speech entitled "Citizenship in a Republic" at the Sorbonne in Paris on April 23, 1910. Here is an excerpt from that speech:

> *It is not the critic who counts; not the man who points out how the strong man stumbles, or where the doer of deeds could have done them better. The credit belongs to the man who is actually in the arena, whose face is marred by dust and sweat and blood; who strives valiantly; who errs, who comes short again and again, because there is no effort without error and shortcoming; but who does actually strive to do the deeds; who knows the great enthusiasms, the great devotions; who spends himself in a worthy cause; who at the best knows in the end the triumph of high achievement, and who at the worst, if he fails, at least fails while daring greatly, so that his place shall never be with those cold and timid souls who neither know victory nor defeat.*

I have found myself "in the arena" throughout my life and truth to be told, I have a hunger for the arena in all facets of my life that stems from my athletic background. I have been in positions in my professional career that are more akin to the "critic." In those instances, I have always felt uncomfortable and out of position. I seek the figurative arena in all that I do and encourage you to do the same.

*Love,*
*Dad*

*Dear Hunter*

A tree doesn't struggle to be a tree; it is naturally a tree. A dog doesn't struggle to be a dog; it is naturally a dog. The world is full of living things that are naturally themselves because they couldn't possibly be anything else. One of the peculiar elements of being human is that most of us spend a lifetime learning how to be ourselves. Why is this so challenging for our species?

Intuitively, you might think that being someone other than our natural self would be more difficult than remaining true to our authentic self, but the reality runs counter to this intuition. As infants and toddlers, we have no problem being our true self; we follow the example of the tree and the dog. However, something happens to us as we age. Each of us suffers the burden of an identity crisis. Addressing this identity crisis is one of the greatest achievements that you can accomplish in your lifetime. Sadly, many people never resolve their identity crisis. Those who do are able to release the weight of this burden and, by doing so, give themselves an opportunity to self-actualize. As Eckhart Tolle wrote in his book, *A New Earth*, "Only the truth of who you are, if realized, will set you free."

I have probably been guilty of saying that you shouldn't worry about what other people think of you. There is some truth to this, but the reality is that as human beings we are social creatures and, therefore, we will always have some concern, if not awareness, of what other people think of us. Throughout my life, if I was posed the question, "How would you want other people to describe you?" my answers would vary at different stages of my life. When I was younger, I would probably have answered that question with adjectives such as *intelligent, insightful, talented,* and *hard-working.* Although I suppose my answer is subject to change because I am still developing and growing, I will tell you that as I write this, there are only two adjectives that I hope people would use to describe me: *kind* and *authentic*. I've come to learn that every other descriptor pales in comparison. In fact, I would go so far as to say that these two adjectives are the only two that are necessary for enlightenment and self-actualization.

Before we can consider how to overcome an identity crisis, perhaps we should explore why some people have this identity crisis in the first place. What happens to us that forces us to hide our authentic self away beyond walls that take a lifetime to tear down? I can only speculate that there is an evolutionary trait that pushes us towards social compliance in an effort to "fit in" with the pack. This forced social compliance manifests itself in peculiar ways. Whether it is part of our DNA or socially programmed into us, I would speculate that almost everyone is cursed with a deep-seated concern that they are, at some level, not good enough. As a result, at a young age we start to act as we think we are expected to act. We start to be the person that we think the world wants us to be. What a losing strategy, and a tragedy of life!

As much as it may be tempting to blame this tendency to act in a way that is not consistent with our authentic self around others, such as parents, teachers, and friends; I'm not convinced that this is fair in all cases. My recollection is that my parents, teachers, and friends accepted me as I was. Outside of some typical teenage peer-pressure, I have no memories of being pressured to be anyone other than me from those closest to me. I think the building of walls around our authentic self comes from internal pressure that is genetically programmed into us, related to fitting in with the tribe. If it's not a genetic predisposition, then I speculate it is more of mystical phenomenon that relates to one of our fundamental life's missions—find yourself and be yourself. As Oscar Wilde said, "Be yourself; everyone else is already taken."

Not only is the freedom of being your authentic self liberating, it directly impacts how others respond to you. Interacting with an authentic person makes us feel safe. Safe in a pre-historic, evolutionary way, but also safe to be our authentic selves in their presence. Ultimately, it is this desire that I believe we all crave. We are starved for signals from our peers that we have permission to be ourselves. It is absolutely amazing how attracted people are to other people that are living as their authentic selves. It's like watching moths to a flame. Consider your favorite musician, your favorite actor, your favorite teacher, or your best friend. I bet they all have at least one thing in common authenticity. You can't fake it, and we may not be able to describe it, but everyone knows it when they see it.

Authenticity is not to be confused with brutal honesty. We all know those people who think that speaking whatever they are thinking is appreciated by everyone. These people are often self-centered and somewhat arrogant. "I am who I am," they say. This is not authenticity. Authenticity, although slightly different for each of us, almost always includes a healthy dose of compassion and vulnerability. If we were discussing these behaviors on a spectrum, I would contend that phony is one end of the spectrum, honest is in the middle, and authentic is on the other end of the spectrum.

Vulnerability, as I mentioned, is a critical part of living an authentic life. When you are living as your authentic self, you will be comfortable saying the following phrases as often as they apply: "I don't know," "I was wrong," "I'm not sure, what do you think?" Phrases like these, combined with outstanding listening skills and comfortable body language, are signals to the recipient that you are open to having genuine conversations. I have observed these signals instantly ratchet up the level of conversation. It seems that people are so longing for authenticity that when they find it, they can't resist the opportunity to open up themselves. I have found my conversations to be much more meaningful and sincere over the years as I have been able to access, even incrementally, my authentic self. It has been quite remarkable to witness.

Compassion is the other necessary ingredient for actualizing your authentic self. It is my belief that one of the central characteristics of being a human being is compassion. I do not believe that compassion is taught. In fact, I think we must be taught to shield ourselves from our natural-born compassion. Demonstrating compassion in all that you do is necessary to signal to others that they have the permission to share their authentic self with you. People are more observant on a subconscious level than we give them credit for. For example, assume that you routinely withhold your compassion when interacting with food service workers or when describing your co-workers to your wife. You are subconsciously creating an emotional obstacle between you and your wife. I understand this may not be your intention, but you are subconsciously signaling that you are not a "safe" place for others to be their authentic self. This is a difficult pill to swallow. *But my friends and family represent my safe space, and sometimes I need to vent about other people to them. If my co-workers are pissing me off, and you're telling me not to share this with my friends and family, aren't you asking me to withhold my authentic self from them?* I understand your point, and I suppose it comes down to how you are expressing yourself. You can complain about someone and still demonstrate compassion towards them, and that is the effort that I am asking you to make. Make allowances for other people's behavior—even when that behavior bothers you. They, too, are fallible human beings trying to find their way through the labyrinth of life. We never really know what internal struggles other people are dealing with, so I am asking you to extend grace to everyone you meet and in the manner in which you talk about other people.

Hunter, I see your authentic self in the two-year-old that you are, and it is beautiful. Truly. You have a zest for life, a curious disposition, a fiercely independent spirit, a kind soul, and a sense of humor that leaves your mother and I in stitches daily. Whether you are reading this at the age of 20 or 80, please reflect upon whether you are allowing your true self to shine through. If not, please work at tearing down the walls that you've built up. You deserve to live your life free from the chains of self-doubt and the world deserves to bask in the light of your true self. Please know that, whether I am with you or not as you read this. Wherever I am, I wish for you to experience the freedom of being the miracle that is you—nothing more and nothing less.

*Love,*
*Dad*

*Dear Hunter*

I'm not going to beat around the bush; I suffer from depression. I've been diagnosed with major depressive disorder since I was 35 and likely have been suffering with this disorder since I was a young adult.

I suppose it goes without saying that I hope that you don't have to experience living with depression or any other form of mental health disorder. However, I would be remiss not to remind you that mental health disorders are genetic. Further, even if you do not suffer from a mental health disorder it is certain that you will have people in your life who do. It is my hope that this letter may lay the foundation for understanding how to deal (or how to deal with others who are afflicted) with mental health disorders.

I've been delaying writing this letter because I knew it would not be easy to do so. However, you need to hear this discussion about mental health as much as you need to hear a discussion about any other topic in this book. Humans have been dealing with mental health issues for at least as long as human existence has been documented. Unfortunately, for most of that time there has been a stigma associated with suffering from mental health issues. Even today, despite all of the progress that has been made, there remains a tacit stigma that I have experienced firsthand.

The human brain is a magnificent miracle. Its ability to process, store, and recall information is mind-boggling; no pun intended. The depth and nuance of emotion that the brain can observe, comprehend, and elicit is what fundamentally separates us from our animal friends. However, it is, like every other part of the body, susceptible to ailments. We understand the ailment of arthritis in our joints. The scientific community has a firm grasp of what it is, what causes it, and how to treat it. Unfortunately, at the time that I am writing this, this is not entirely the case with our brains. Our current knowledge of the human brain remains a frontier of our  scientific community that has much more to reveal to us than we presently understand. Suffice to say, a large and growing percent of the population suffers from some form of mental health ailment. For some, this ailment may be a minor inconvenience; for others it can be debilitating. For many, the consequences of mental health disorders tend to oscillate between these extremes. This is where I fall.

There have been times in my life when I have been completely overwhelmed by depression, where getting out of bed or basic hygiene was a mountain too steep to climb. There have been other times in my life when I barely noticed my depression. However, it is always there. Depression has been compared to having a black dog as a pet that follows you everywhere. Sometimes the dog is small, quiet, and well-behaved, and other times it is the size of a bear, loud and rambunctious. Either way, it is always with you. Others have described depression as living underneath a dark rain cloud which size varies. Sometimes, the cloud is a mere wisp of fog. Other days, the cloud is tremendously threatening and launching lightning bolts into your brain. Either way, it is always with you.

Mustering the courage to get help was not easy for me. Throughout my life, I felt the presence of depression but never understood that it was a physical ailment for which I could seek assistance. I was always inclined to find reasons why I wasn't feeling "well." The first major depressive episode that I endured was when I was at Rutgers University as a sophomore in college. Life was treating me well by most external measures. I was performing well in school. I had a great group of friends. I should have been enjoying a relatively stress-free period of my life. However, I began to suffocate under the weight of what I now know was depression. Because I didn't understand that depression doesn't always have a "reason," I made up reasons that I felt the way I did. To make matters worse, I sought solace in alcohol. I actually did seek out professional help from a counselor at the school, but she made me feel like a fraud and worse; she made me feel weak. She couldn't have been more disinterested in helping me or listening to me. I wish I had the maturity and perspective to realize that either I caught her on a bad day or she wasn't a particularly effective counselor. I wish I had the courage to seek help from someone else. Instead, I just assumed that help was not to be found.

Further, I assumed that the depression—or whatever was causing me to feel the way that I felt—was my fault. If you take nothing away from this letter, please take this. Mental health disorders are NOT the fault of the person suffering. If you broke your leg or developed asthma, you wouldn't think less of yourself. However, when it comes to mental health, it is challenging to get the person who is suffering to recognize that the brain can suffer ailments as any other body part can. We stigmatize ourselves even before the world stigmatizes us. Of course, it is worth mentioning that not every time you feel sad or anxious, you should assume that you are suffering from a mental health disorder. As a human being you will experience a wide range of emotions in your life; some will be pleasurable emotions, and some will be painful ones. This is natural. At the risk of giving you the idea that you can self-diagnose yourself, I will tell you to be on the lookout for a pattern of negative emotions that don't have a rational source. For example, if your girlfriend breaks your heart and you feel sad—this is normal, not a symptom of depression. In fact, there is a big difference between feeling depressed and having a medically diagnosed condition. Without the benefit of mental health training, you may not be able to discern the difference. There is nothing wrong with seeking help to find out. If your leg ached to the extent that it was impacting the quality of your life, would you seek medical attention? I would hope so. Treat your mental health similarly.

It would be another 16 years before I sought help again. During these 16 years, I continued to live in a mental environment that oscillated between harrowing and healthy. In retrospect, I can't believe it was that long. I sought help again because I had to. I was out of options. The weight of my depression was sending my mind to dark places that I knew were dangerous. I spent the next several years attending to my mental health in earnest. I saw numerous doctors until I found ones that I was comfortable with. In addition to the medication that I was prescribed, I learned coping strategies such as biofeedback, mindfulness, and deep breathing that I would have scoffed at years ago but have come to rely upon to fight off the dragons of depression that I have accepted will come and go for the rest of my life. By far, the biggest obstacle that I faced in getting real and actionable help for my condition was recognizing that the best time to work on your mental health is not in the middle of a depressive episode. Intellectually, it should come as no surprise that your brain is not operating at its sharpest when it is injured. Emotionally, we struggle with this reality. When would be the best time to strengthen your leg muscles—when your leg was feeling healthy? Or when it hurts so badly that you can't walk? The same is true for your mind.

Lastly, I will leave you with a note about compassion and empathy. If anyone deserves your compassion and empathy, it is yourself. I, unfortunately, was very hard on myself when suffering through episodes of depression, which didn't make the situation better, and reflected my ignorance of the subject. I know you want to be mentally healthy. If you don't feel that way, it is not for lack of trying. Don't berate yourself for thoughts that may be out of your control. Similarly, mental health may not be as obvious as a visible wound, but the pain can be just as real. Therefore, remember to consider this when you interact with the world. You never know who is fighting demons in their own mind. Provide your fellow (wo)man the benefit of the doubt whenever you are inclined not to. Someday, you may need them to do the same for you.

*Love,*
*Dad*

*Dear Hunter*

Life is a miraculous and beautiful gift, and it is also a mystery. Who or what bestowed this gift upon us? Where did life come from? What existed before life, and why? Why are we here? Where do we go after life on Earth? The questions are endless and can easily lead into an existential crisis if you think too deeply about them. Coming to terms with these questions is the most personal thought process of your lifetime. We are all in the same boat filled with the same doubts and fears, but none of us know the answers. We can speculate. We can believe. We can trust. However, there is no one who can tell you the "right" answer.

Many people find the answers to these questions in their religious faith. Personally, my religious faith has ebbed and flowed throughout my life. There are times when I find the idea of an all-powerful and all-knowing entity overseeing our lives impossible to comprehend. There are other times when I find the converse idea of the absence of such a being impossible to comprehend. Perhaps the best that I can conclude is that the power, being, or God is not something I'll ever comprehend. Try to imagine a shape existing in four physical dimensions. I doubt you can. Does that mean that existence cannot occur in four physical dimensions or just that our brain can't comprehend it? On my most faithful days, I find solace in the Christian God. On my least faithful days, I find myself agnostic at best. I wish I could paint a different picture of my faith for you. I wish I could tell you that I am fully faithful to our God the Almighty Father, but I'm not that strong . . . yet.

I grew up in a Catholic family. I dutifully attended church every Sunday, followed by Sunday school. I learned about the Bible and its teachings. I learned about the life, death, and resurrection of Jesus Christ. I learned about sin, heaven, and hell. I prayed, kneeling, beside my bed every night. I memorized the Lord's Prayer, the Apostles Creed, and the Hail Mary. I was far from perfect in living in accordance with Biblical edicts, but learned to keep track of my failures and confess them to the priest at Saint Anthony's during the sacrament of confession. Everyone I knew was of the Catholic faith. I had no reason to believe that everything that I was learning was anything but the known truth.

It was a hot and humid summer day in 1984. I was ten years old. I had just returned from a day of swimming and playing stickball at the public pool. I rode my blue Huffy bike from the pool to my home, but not before stopping at Uncle Tony's Stationary store to buy myself two packs of baseball cards, a copy of Baseball Digest with Leon Durham on the cover, and a roll of Necco Wafer candies. As I entered the kitchen of our second-floor apartment, I heard an unfamiliar sound emanating from my parents' bedroom. My mother (your grandma) who was eight months pregnant with your Uncle Joey, was laying on her bed sobbing with her back towards the partially cracked door. I quietly entered the room and laid down next to her. Although no one had told me just how sick my grandma was, I knew she was sick, and I somehow knew what had happened. "Did Grandma die?" I whispered. Your grandma confirmed my intuition through her muffled cries. I didn't stay with her long. As quietly as I entered; I left her room and climbed the stairs to my bedroom.

I remember placing my baseball cards, the Baseball Digest, and the Necco Wafers on my bed. I took a deep thoughtful breath. Then, my heart leapt with joy. *She did it! Grandma made it to heaven!!* I was so excited for her. As we learned in Sunday School class, heaven was a paradise. There were no tears, no pain, no illness, and no worries. Heaven was the ultimate reward for a life well-lived. Grandma earned her spot there—that was for sure. She was beyond kind, loving, and faithful. Amidst my excitement, I was hit with a wave of confusion.

*Why was my mother so sad? Why was my mother crying? Were they tears of joy? They didn't feel like tears of joy.* In the days that followed, I observed my family's mourning of my grandma and the predominant emotion of the family was sadness. My grandma's passing represented the loss of my innocence in the matter of life and death. It was clear to me that no one in my family really knew what happened to us after death. Yes, they had their faith, but their faith was imperfect, as I have come to learn all faith is. This genuinely frightened me. If these adults didn't know for sure what happens to someone after death, how was I supposed to know? Adults are supposed to know everything. *Who was going to tell me what to believe? Who should I listen to? Somebody must know, right?*

I'll never forget that experience. It left me with questions that remain unanswered to this day. As much as I wish I had answers to all the world's mysteries for my own knowledge and peace of mind; I wish I had answers for you. It pains me to think about you having to deal with a loss of this magnitude without being able to provide you with the answers that will take away the pain that death can bring. I can't now and likely will never be able to. Dealing with death is one of the loneliest feelings that I have felt because there is no one on Earth who can explain it to me. Although I haven't learned the answers to these questions about existence, life, and death, I have learned how to make peace(ish) with my ignorance.

This peace has come to me primarily through prayer. When I say "prayer," I am not referring exclusively to the conventional definition of prayer. In my opinion, anytime you convene with the universe mentally, you are praying. I truly do believe in the power of prayer. I can't explain it. I can't comprehend it. But I truly believe that the universe is listening and, perhaps more importantly, the universe is talking. For most of my life my prayers were a one-way conversation. I would talk and hope that the universe was listening. In my mid-30s,

I recall listening to a pastor discuss prayer during a Sunday service. He encouraged us to think of prayer as our means of communicating with God and reminded us that all effective communication is a two-way street. He further posed a question, "If you believe that you are having a conversation with the creator of the universe, the all-knowing and benevolent God who is capable of teaching you more than your brain could even comprehend; who is doing most of the talking and why?"

This Socratic question really struck a chord with me. My prayer and meditation have never been the same. I really do spend my time listening . . . intently. Although there are times when I wish the responses were readily decipherable, I have found peace and wisdom through this practice that I don't believe could have been obtained any other way. The universe will speak to you—it may not be loud, it may not be in English, it may not be often, but with patience and persistence; I promise you that you will hear and feel a comforting message that will move you closer to understanding the mysteries of life and death.

For every beginning there is an ending. I don't know of any exceptions to this. I've heard the expression—don't be sad because it's over, be grateful that it happened. I've applied this saying many times in my life. Watching you develop as a toddler has reminded me just how true this expression is. For example, last Saturday we went walking in the snow together. We were outside for hours as you toddled around in your snowsuit. We built snowmen. We made and threw snowballs. I watched you taste more snow than I ever saw anyone eat. Eventually, it was time to go back inside. You were shivering head to toe and so was I. However, getting you back in the house was no easy feat. You've heard of toddler temper tantrums? Well, this was the mother of all tantrums—legs kicking, arms flailing, and screaming at the top of your lungs. Once inside, you stood at the front door with your hands on the handle screaming for "more snow." My heart was breaking for you, but I also knew that you were sad because we had so much fun, and you didn't want it to end. This life snapshot reminded me of our journey on Earth. Don't be sad because it's over—be grateful that it happened.

*Love,*
*Dad*

*Dear Hunter*

My younger brother—your Uncle Joey, in addition to being a tremendous human being, was one of the greatest athletes to come out of our hometown of Hawthorne, New Jersey. He has amazing God-given athletic abilities combined with a work ethic that has no peer. Joey could, and did, excel at any sport that man had organized. His passion was baseball. From the time Joey was old enough to hold a baseball bat, he was in love with the sport. Almost every memory I have of Joey involves baseball. He quickly developed a reputation in our town as a baseball phenom. Being ten years older than Joey, I didn't get to see him play as much as I would have liked to, but I remember the times that I did like it was yesterday. I was in awe. From a very early age, everyone who watched him play had the same, although often unspoken, assessment. *This kid could play in the major leagues someday.*

As he aged, his passion and love for the sport grew along with his abilities. In my letter to you about sports, I mentioned the sacrifices I made in my youth for my athletic endeavors. These sacrifices pale in comparison to those Joey made . His high school summers were spent on travelling baseball teams, his winters were spent working out in the gym, and his social life took a back seat to his baseball commitments. Joey had no plan B. In fact, this was an intentional decision that he made. I recall him saying that a plan B would give him an excuse not to devote all of his resources towards his dream. He was all-in in the pursuit of his dream of becoming a professional baseball player.

As predicted, Joey's baseball career was on a rocket trajectory towards the big leagues. He attended Wagner College and excelled in the Division I baseball conference as the team's shortstop. His college baseball career was not absent of challenges, including a nearly career-ending injury to his eye. However, Joey would not be deterred. His grit and determination would not allow it. I will never forget the day of the 2007 Major League Baseball draft. I was deployed to the Pacific Ocean on the nuclear fast-attack submarine, the USS Key West (SSN-722). As luck would have it, we were operating on the surface on the day of the draft and, therefore, I had internet access. I could remotely participate in the overwhelming joy my family felt when Joey was drafted in the 42nd round by the Baltimore Orioles. I can't describe the joy and elation that I felt in response to this news with words. I can only imagine how he felt. This was the defining moment of a lifetime pursuit. Most kids only dream of being drafted by a major league baseball team—Joey was living every schoolboy's fantasy.

Joey played one season plus a spring training in the minor league system for the Baltimore Orioles before being cut by the team. As I can only imagine how Joey felt when being drafted the year before, I can, again, only imagine how he felt when let go. When I heard the news, I was not disappointed or sad. The only emotions I felt were compassion and empathy for what my brother must have been feeling. I had never met anyone in my life who had worked harder for something than Joey had for baseball. I can only assume that the weeks, months, and maybe years that followed for Joey were akin to mourning the loss of a loved one. Joey was forced to let go of a dream and start over.

Your Uncle Joey is as resilient a person as they come. He built his life from scratch after baseball. Joey never had a plan B, so now he would have to create another plan A. He was, in some sense, back to the drawing board. After some soul searching and several wrong turns, Joey attended and graduated from the police academy. He is currently a detective with the Hawthorne Police Department, and he serves the community in which we were raised with bravery and valor.

Why do I share this story about Uncle Joey with you? Because I want you to know that sometimes in life, we have to start over. Setbacks are a natural part of life, but it certainly doesn't feel natural when you live through one. No one wants to start over. No one likes the feeling of having lost or wasted time to make up for. However, it is more common than not, and I would predict that you will find yourself in a "back to the drawing board" situation at some point in your life. When this happens to you, please do not despair. You are not alone. I, too, have had my share of setbacks. Examples include: I left a full academic scholarship at Rutgers University. I ended my career in the United States Navy because of an injury. I was asked to resign from an executive-level position for reasons that were never disclosed to me. I have lived through a marital divorce. With the exception of my unexpected retirement from the United States Navy, none of these other setbacks created an existential crisis for me similar to Joey's. However, the accumulation of life setbacks has taught me some lessons about finding peace even amid disappointments. I'd like to share these lessons with you.

- Nothing can send you back to square zero. Even if life circumstances are such that you feel like you have to start over, you never truly do. The experiences, the wisdom, and the life lessons that you gained can never be taken away from you. Joey may have felt like he was starting life over, but his understanding of teamwork, work ethic, and determination have served him well beyond his baseball career. Take inventory of what you learned and what you will take with you in the aftermath of a setback.

- The flip side of starting over is letting go. The most challenging part of letting go is usually not the fear of losing what we have, but rather the fear of the unknown. Not knowing what comes next can be a frightening experience, especially if you were previously on a well-known path. It is my experience that the unknown is never as bad as we are inclined to believe it will be. As humans, we do not deal well with uncertainty. This is precisely the reason that so many people refuse to make changes in their lives when all rational thought would lead them to do so. People will often choose to remain in toxic work environments or relationships because they are afraid of the shadow that the monster of uncertainty casts.

- Never allow your self-identity to be uniquely defined by an external factor or role. This is easier said than done. I'm sure Joey's identity was tied to his role as a baseball player, just as my identity was tied directly to my role as a naval officer. However, the reality is that your self-identity can never be taken from you if you cultivate that identity based on your character rather than your role. No one and no circumstance can strip you of your self-identity without your permission. Your roles in life will come and go. The earlier you accept that fact, the earlier you can start building a self-identity independent of your position and tied directly to your character.

- Face setbacks with a sense of curiosity instead of fear. Every setback in my lifetime, I have come to be thankful for after time. As one door closes in life, another door opens. This is more than just a platitude; I believe this to be true. As much as you can, be excited and enthusiastic about stepping through that newly opened door. The universe has never disappointed me.

- The only constant in life is change. Learn to appreciate the present, but know that it will quickly dissolve into the past. We have no reasonable expectation that tomorrow will be the same as today. This is one of the reasons that life is so exciting and miraculous. I've found life to be much more akin to a roller coaster than a riverboat cruise. Learn to embrace the highs and endure the lows without feeling an emotional attachment to your circumstances.

- Time heals all wounds. There will be setbacks in your life that cut so deeply that you will be inconsolable . . . for a time. Give yourself permission to feel the pain that comes with setbacks, but remind yourself that the pain is temporary. Know that things may get worse before they get better. Further, time can move extremely slowly when you are hurting. Acknowledge these truths, but remind yourself that you will get over it. You will live to fight another day. You will come out on the other side, victorious.

*Love,*
*Dad*

*Dear Hunter*

If you can believe it, I grew up without social media. In fact, I grew up without the internet. I know that this means your old man is quite literally an "old man." It also means that my generation, Generation X, is unique in that although we grew up without the internet, we were the first generation to embrace it. I remember that I got my first computer with internet access in 1992. There wasn't much on the world wide web then. However, over the years, I watched and participated in the evolution of the internet. I had a front-row seat for it all—message boards, email, chat, websites, online shopping, social media, smartphones, and texting. The world had arguably changed more in 20 years than it had in the previous two hundred. Of all the changes that were ushered into existence by this new technology, I have found social media to have the most profound impact on how we, as humans, interact with each other.

The benefits of social media are ubiquitous. Never before has the world been smaller. Never before have we been able to remain in contact with our friends and family from all over the globe in such an intimate and daily fashion. Never before have we been able to find and interact with our "tribe" so effortlessly. We have the ability to share our lives, express our thoughts, and find like-minded people with an ease that would have been unthinkable a mere 20 years ago. However, you don't upend thousands of years of human interaction virtually overnight without some untoward and unintended consequences.

When Facebook became popular circa 2011, I was enamored with it. I was an early adopter of the ability to connect with long-lost friends and acquaintances. I posted photos of my life highlights, engaged with friends and family, and even discussed and debated politics. I was, in a sense, drunk with this new-found ability to interact with people from the comfort of my living room couch. However, I was failing to take into account a few of the dynamics of social media engagement. For example, posting highlights, photos, and videos of your life can be nice to share but can easily be perceived as being boastful. I am sure that I was guilty of this. This was a problem for several reasons. For starters, no one likes a boastful person. And in my case, I didn't want to be a boastful person. It wasn't my intent, but every action has unintended consequences. Additionally, when you come across as a braggart on social media, you can and will drive a wedge between you and your friends. Ironically, using the tool that was meant to bring people together can actually divide people. This usually occurs silently. If 20 percent of your friends on a social media platform are responding positively to your posts, it is natural to assume that you are positively engaging with your friends. However, what about the other 80 percent? Just because they are not "saying" anything doesn't mean they aren't watching. If you are not actively preventing yourself from bragging on social media about your life, you probably are. This is a peculiar phenomenon, but one worth exploring.

Resisting the temptation to measure our lives against the yardstick of others' lives is challenging to say the least. Social media exaggerates this tendency because we aren't actually seeing into other people's true lives, but it gives us the impression that we are. More specifically, we end up comparing our lives, which are full of bumps, bruises, and scars, with the highlight reel of other people's lives. This is a recipe for a mental health disaster. No one is living a perfect life. Everyone I know is struggling with something, but social media tends to present us with a perspective that would imply the contrary. This is relevant in two ways. The first is the importance of being cognizant of this when sharing information about your life on social media. I don't want to imply that you shouldn't be proud of your life, your achievements, and your activities, but be careful about shouting them from the rooftops of social media platforms. You have friends that may be struggling financially, personally, professionally, mentally, or spiritually who are likely to see your posts and compare their life to your highlight reel. Is this your responsibility? Not directly, but these are your friends, right? You wouldn't intentionally do anything to hurt those you hold most dear. There may be an unavoidable element to this phenomenon that you can do nothing about, outside of sharing nothing. However, I believe you would be remiss to not consider how your social media engagement may be making your network feel. Strive for inclusion, positivity, and engagement. The second way is the flip side of the first. Specifically, avoid the trap of comparing your own life to other people's highlight reels. It is not an apples-to-apples comparison and nothing good occurs in the depths of this mental trap.

Social media is the world's largest cocktail party. Imagine a huge ballroom with all of your friends, family, and acquaintances in attendance. Additionally, all their friends, family, and acquaintances are also in attendance. And their... et cetera, et cetera. I have found that the behavior that you would exhibit at this fictitious cocktail party is a good standard to apply to how you behave on social media. If, at the cocktail party, there was a microphone available to address the crowd, how would you use it? If you wouldn't feel comfortable, outside of a healthy fear of public speaking, saying or sharing something there, you probably should think twice about sharing it on social media. Similarly, if you came upon a group of your friends discussing politics, how would you feel comfortable expressing your opinion to that group? Again, if you wouldn't say it in public in front of all of your family and friends, don't say it on social media.

From 2009 through 2013, I was very active on social media in a manner that extended beyond friends and family. As a political candidate and a radio talk show host, I was putting myself and my content out into the wild west of social media. As I found out the hard way, you need thick skin to do this, and for the majority of the time that I was "out there", my skin wasn't nearly as thick as it needed to be. This was especially true during my run for Congress in 2012. My candidacy was based on honesty, transparency, and commonsense change. I wasn't professing hatred towards anyone. I wasn't advocating for radical or threatening policy changes. I was pleasantly surprised at how my campaign platform was supported by my friends, my family, and the people I met along the campaign trail. However, social media was a separate animal for which I was not prepared. The vitriol that was thrown my way on social media by strangers was shocking. I was cursed at, ridiculed, and mocked more during that campaign than I had been cumulatively in my lifetime. I had close friends who encouraged me to ignore these comments. "Don't feed the trolls," they wisely advised. I couldn't do it. I wasn't strong enough. I was engaging with strangers daily, trying to make the case that they had unfairly categorized me. I was pleading my case to strangers who seemed to thrive on the drama. My efforts, although well-intentioned, created a feeding frenzy at my own expense.

I learned a lot about handling criticism from that experience, especially as it relates to criticism from strangers on social media. The number one takeaway was to expect criticism, sometimes vicious criticism, when you put yourself "out there." The only way to avoid pointed, hateful, and public mockery is to keep your head down and avoid taking online risks. As Aristotle said, "Criticism is something we can avoid easily by saying nothing, doing nothing, and being nothing." This is the one and only way to avoid the criticism. As I am writing this book, I know now that I will have to endure online criticisms. I can hear the comments in my head already. *Drivel. Amateur. Mundane. Cliche.* To be honest, it hurts my feelings just thinking about it. However, I remind myself that this is the unavoidable price of reaching for your goals and dreams. I've been told, "If you don't know them personally, don't take their criticisms personally." This is easy to say and difficult to do. However,, most endeavors worthy of pursuit are difficult. Pursuing your dreams is no exception.

Social media is a revolutionary move forward for humanity. I truly believe this. If used with a dose of humility, consideration, and empathy, its value far outweighs its downsides. Ultimately, social media simply increases our ability to communicate and engage with our communities of friends, family, and those with shared interests, but it should never be an excuse to violate or forget the standards of respect and courtesy upon which effective human communication is built.

*Love,*
*Dad*

*Dear Hunter*

The ability to share your thoughts and ideas with others through the written word is an ability that is uniquely human. Many animals communicate, but only humans craft their communication in a format that is captured forever. The written word can educate or entertain. It can elicit tears or laughter. Although the same can be said for the spoken word, it is a fallacy to reduce the concept of the written word to the mere transcription of the spoken word.

The written word is a language unto itself. Learning a new language requires practice, patience, and persistence. The written word is also an art form unto itself. Expressing yourself with artistic skill requires creativity, curiosity, and courage. The best writing creates the illusion that the writer has effortlessly translated thoughts into words. Many people are fooled by this illusion and, as a consequence, find writing intimidating because they can't duplicate this effortless translation from thought to word.

My experience is that writing is anything but effortless. Even on my best days, writing is a harrowing uphill climb through the places in my mind where I ordinarily dare not tread. I believe that F. Scott Fitzgerald was spot on when he said, "All good writing is swimming underwater and holding your breath." I agree.

Why is writing well so challenging? Most of us don't find conversing challenging. Isn't writing just capturing and writing what you would say aloud? It is true that when we converse with someone, we are converting our thoughts to words, which is similar to writing. However, what we are lacking is the feedback mechanism of conversation that guides our thoughts and steers the dialogue. The verbal ping-pong of a conversation is effortless for most people. However, when we write, there is no one to listen to our words as we formulate them. I'm sure you've experienced awkward silences in conversation. Well,, writing is one long awkward silence that the writer must learn to make peace with. Further, the expectations for writing are higher than in a casual conversation. The reader, who is often a stranger, lends you their time in exchange for knowledge, excitement, surprise, or intrigue. The reader pulls up a chair, folds his arms, leans back, and says, "Entertain me." The writer doesn't want to disappoint this reader, so the writer thinks, re-thinks, and thinks some more; the pressure builds, and this pressure blocks all creative juices. However, even when the reader is removed from the equation, the challenges remain. The process of writing for your own benefit, such as journaling, is also an uphill battle for most people.

Given the enormous stressors and challenges, why write at all? That is a fair question and one that only you can answer. For me, writing weakens the fear of my own mortality. Theology aside, the thought of vanishing from existence scares me. Writing provides me with a feeling, if not an illusion, of immortality. My flesh may not live forever, but my words might. Related, writing provides me with a connection to humanity for which I have not found a substitute. Writing affords me the opportunity to engage with a wider population than afforded by my everyday life. The desire to interact with other people is innate. We want to tell our story. We want to be heard. For the writer, these wants are deep-seated needs. For a writer, writing scratches an itch that must be scratched. A writer writes because he has to. A writer writes because he has something to say that must be said. A writer writes to connect with the world in a way that he otherwise couldn't.

Make no mistake, I am still learning how to write. I anticipate that I will consider myself a student of the written word to my dying day. As such, I feel reluctant to provide writing advice, but at the risk of posing as a teacher, I will share some writing tactics that have served me well.

- Be curious and inquisitive. An open mind is the most powerful tool in the writer's toolbox. You have more than 6,000 unique thoughts daily that flutter about in your mind like beautiful butterflies. Curiosity is the skill of capturing these butterflies gently enough so as not to harm them, but assertively enough to examine them. If you can capture and examine one fleeting thought a day, you will have a lifetime of material about which to write.

- Get out of your own way. In the context of baseball, Yogi Berra said, "You can't hit and think at the same time." I have found the same to be true of writing. As counterintuitive as it may sound, I write best when I am able to turn my brain off. When I say "brain," I am referring to the analytical part of my brain. This part of the brain is responsible for the pestering, negative self-talk that we are all so familiar with. *You are no good. Your writing sucks. Give up.* Performing with the volume of this voice turned down is often called "flow." Athletes, singers, and artists strive to attain this state of mind because they find, without exception, that this state optimizes performance and the enjoyment they find in their craft. Developing a practice of meditation and mindfulness is the best way that I know to train the mind to work in the flow. At the risk of oversimplifying an ancient practice, I would contend that a daily practice of meditation serves mostly to quiet the background noise of our minds.

- Slow down, but don't stop. When it comes to writing, I would echo the words of Martin Luther King, Jr.: "If you can't fly then run, if you can't run then walk, if you can't walk then crawl, but whatever you do you have to keep moving forward." Writing is a game of momentum. Many people fail at this game because they mistakenly think that writing is a game of motivation. Believing in this fallacy is the writer's kiss of death. If you are a writer, you must write. I have failed in this regard throughout my life. The lesson that I have learned over and again is that the only solution to a lack of inspiration or motivation is to write while uninspired and unmotivated. Action is the fuel of the motivation engine.

- Start in the middle. Often, writers will stare at a blank page for hours while attempting to craft their introduction. The blinking cursor on the white background taunts them while they contemplate the meaning of life and the incomprehensible size of the universe. Starting a book, a story, or a chapter is one of the more daunting stages of writing. When you find yourself stuck, jump to the middle. Circle back to the beginning when you're ready. Your readers don't know or care which parts of your writing were written first.

- Give your future self momentum to work with. It is tempting to write until you run out of gas. This is especially true when you are in the flow. I understand. However, as I mentioned, writing is a momentum game. Do your best to leave yourself momentum to work with. Doing so requires a willingness to stop writing when you have a good idea of where you are going with your current momentum. Consider handing the baton to your future self so that he doesn't have to start without any momentum.

- Read. Read. Read. As Stephen King said, "If you don't have time to read, you don't have the time (or the tools) to write. Simple as that." Writing is a craft that is honed principally through two paths: writing and reading. I've never heard of an NFL quarterback who doesn't watch films of other quarterbacks, or a singer that doesn't listen to other singers, or an actor that doesn't watch movies. People who are serious about their craft absorb as much information as they can to prepare themselves to perform. Writing is no different. I would encourage you to read as much as you can. Reading as a writer, however, is different than reading as a non-writer. Observe how the author weaves the tale. Take note of the details: What words are used? What words are not used? What literary devices are used most powerfully? Cherry-pick what appeals to you as a reader and incorporate these strategies in your own works.

- Writing without a deadline is like traveling across town on a stationary bike. You will spin your wheels, but you'll never get there. Most people produce more writing in one year of their formal education than they have cumulatively since. Deadlines work because they prevent the perfectionist inside of us from indefinitely delaying the completion of a project because "it is not good enough yet." Perfection is the enemy of completion. Give yourself a deadline for every writing project you have. Protect yourself from your internal perfectionist.

In the words of Benjamin Franklin, "Either write something worth reading or do something worth writing." I encourage you to do both.

*Love,*
*Dad*

*Dear Hunter*

William James, the great American philosopher, psychologist, and physician once said, "We don't laugh because we are happy, we are happy because we laugh." Most of the greatest times in my life were accompanied by laughter. I think back to my high school and college days. My friends and I would sit around and make each other laugh for hours on end. I think back to my submarine days; sometimes the only way to make extended submerged deployments palpable was with laughter. I don't think I was aware of this during those times, but I now realize that laughing is truly one of the greatest and simplest pleasures in life.

Often, the greatest pleasures in life are the most challenging to define. Humor is an example. What is humor? The quality of being amusing or comical. What does that mean? Ask yourself this—If you watch a video of someone tripping and falling on their face, do you find that funny? Most people do. But why? I have found this question very challenging to answer. What makes something funny? Philosophers, scientists, and comedians have been trying to answer this question for centuries. There are many theories, but I tend to agree with E.B. White who said, "Humor can be dissected, as a frog can. But the thing dies in the process and the innards are discouraging to any but the purely scientific mind." Comedy is an art, not a science. It is not governed by steadfast rules. You might find something funny that I find repulsive. Our sense of humor is a unique personality characteristic that varies from person to person. The explanation of humor may be a mystery, but its benefits are clear and understood.

Humor can keep you grounded. As you age, you may feel pressure to act serious and sophisticated. This is natural. It would be difficult to hold positions of authority while acting like an elementary school clown. However, never allow yourself to take life so seriously that you can't laugh at yourself. I've observed people who seem to think that if they show a sense of humor, they are diminishing their own importance. I feel truly sorry for these people. Regardless of what position in life you may obtain, that position is temporary, but your role as a human being is permanent. Humor, especially self-deprecating humor, signals to others that you have a well-balanced and humble approach to life.

Humor can put people at ease. I recall meeting the General in command of the Central Command, or CENTCOM, in Bahrain in 2003. Tensions were high in the region. Those of us who were serving in the Middle East felt substantial daily pressure. The General met with the troops to discuss the status of operations in Iraq and Afghanistan. We were gathered in military formation and were standing at attention. Like it was yesterday, I remember watching him stride to the podium. He looked out at the troops standing before him for a moment or two. He then proceeded to tell a series of jokes. *A horse walks into a bar and the bartender says, "Why the long face?"* Not the world's funniest joke, but the joke elicited some polite, yet nervous, laughter from the troops. He continued. *A chameleon walks into a bar and the bartender says, "If your wife calls, I didn't see you."* More laughter from the troops, this time a bit more relaxed. He continued. *A termite walks into a bar and asks, "Is the bar tender here?"* This one had a delayed response because it takes a second to get the joke, especially when delivered verbally, but the troops were flat out laughing now. We were in the middle of a war, thousands of miles from our homes, family, and friends but this general had us laughing with a series of relatively stupid jokes. He successfully broke the tension, and had us relaxed and better positioned mentally to receive his serious and sobering message regarding the war.

Humor can help you connect with people. The General not only broke the tension, he connected with us. There we were, hundreds of troops from all different walks of life. Yet, with a few stupid jokes, he connected with us all. I don't know of another tool that has the power to connect diverse groups of people better than humor. I highly recommend always having a few good jokes in your hip pocket. You will inevitably find yourself in awkward or unfamiliar situations with other people, and a good joke can provide you with an immediate bond. Even a joke that falls flat can be successful in connecting with other people. Humor, and even attempted humor, signals to other people that beneath your exterior lives the soul of another human being.

Humor can heal. Is laughter, in fact, the best medicine? I don't know, but it is certainly a medicine. The mind-body connection is strong. When you find yourself lying in bed with a physical or mental ailment, find something to make yourself laugh. Laughter releases chemicals in the brain that can help your heart pump more evenly, boost your immune system, increase your energy level, and improve your mood. This discussion reminds me of something comedian Jack Handey wrote in *Deep Thoughts*: "Dad always thought laughter was the best medicine. Which I guess is why several of us died of tuberculosis."

Humor can sharpen your mind. For three years, I was enrolled in improvisational comedy classes. I learned a lot about myself and about comedy during those years. The most important thing that I learned is that being funny is not about being the wittiest or craziest person in the room. Most good comedy comes from being a great listener and an astute observer. Learning to improve your listening skills while remaining fully present to what is being said is simple, but it is not easy. Our brains tend to filter information at the expense of really listening to what is being said and observing what is really happening. More specifically, our brains will tend to categorize words and observations based on our previous experiences. I suppose our brains do this in an attempt to conserve brain power. For example, someone starts telling you a story about their recent trip to the DMV. Your brain will tend to reduce its attention to the story because it assumes it already knows the details. *Oh, yes. I've heard this before. The DMV sucks because it is inefficient, the employees are rude, and the wait is long.* However, I encourage you to fight this tendency and really listen to what is being said.

Humor can be funny and clean. There are plenty of people who disagree with me on this, and I understand why. I often laugh at dirty jokes, but I have found that you never really know how other people will respond. Further, I think dirty humor is a lazy form of comedy. Anyone can get a laugh with profanity-laced toilet humor. That's easy. It takes more effort and a more refined sense of humor to get a laugh from a clean joke.

Humor doesn't have to hurt. For all of its positive benefits, humor can cut deep if used inappropriately. The best guidance I can give you is to avoid the temptation to make jokes at another's expense. You may get a laugh from others, you may even get a laugh from the person that you are targeting, but the laughs are not worth it—especially if you are targeting someone's appearance, physical characteristics, race, or sex. As an example of humor cutting deep, when I was younger I was very skinny and had a very bad case of acne. I was the butt of skinny and acne jokes my entire life, even from close family and friends. Did I laugh with them? Most of the time, yes, I did. But their jokes really stung me emotionally. I was very self-conscious about these physical characteristics. Every time someone started to kid me about it, my defenses went up, and I thought *Oh, great. Here we go again.* The truth is, it took years for my self-esteem to heal from the cumulation of these "jokes." Resist the temptation to be the reason why someone's self-esteem suffers. The best humor builds people up and the worst humor tears them down. When employing humor, choose wisely.

*Love,*
*Dad*

P.S. Here are two jokes to keep in your back pocket if you should need them.

***

A man is interviewing for an executive position with a Fortune 500 company. He has successfully made it through the first several rounds of interviews and is in his final interview with the company CEO and the senior vice president of human resources. The CEO asks the man, "What would you say is your biggest weakness?" The man takes a few beats to consider his answer and then responds, "Honesty. Honesty is my biggest weakness." The CEO furrows his brow and says, "I wouldn't think that honesty was a weakness. That sounds more like a strength to me." The man looks the CEO in the eyes and says, "I don't give a damn what you think."

***

Three men have been stranded on a deserted island for years. One day, a lamp washes ashore. The men clean it up and while they are rubbing it clean, a genie emerges from the lamp. The genie tells the men that he is a magical genie and has the power to grant them three wishes. However, since there are three of them, each man will be given one wish. The first man speaks up immediately. "I miss my family so much. I wish I was back home with my family." The genie snaps his fingers and *poof* the man vanishes. The second man says, "I miss my family as well. I wish I was back home with them." *Poof* The man disappears. The third man says to the genie, "Well, I don't have a family. I'm going to have to think about this for a while." The genie tells him to take his time. The man spends the next few days contemplating his options. Then, he says to the genie, "I don't know what to do. There are so many thoughts running through my head." The genie says, "Take your time. You get only one wish, so make it a good one." The man sighs and laments, "I've been stranded on this island with those other two guys for so many years. I've grown accustomed to relying on them. I wish they were still here to help me decide what to do."

*Dear Hunter*

I was about seven years old. It was a bright summer day at the town's public pool. I was hanging out by the tennis courts. Doing what? I don't remember. A boy my age who I had never seen before approached me and said, "My name is Steven. Do you want to be friends?" I considered the question for about a tenth of a second and responded, "Yes! My name is Matt." "Let's go swimming," Steven said. We ran to the pool together and had a great day swimming, playing catch with a tennis ball, and getting to know each other. Although we didn't go to the same school, Steven and I did become friends. We were on the same little league baseball team and are even connected on Facebook to this day. Making friends was so simple back then.

The connotation of the word *friend* evolves as we age. As an elementary school child, I recall my grandmother telling me that you should consider yourself blessed if you have one or two close friends as an adult. I remember scoffing at that notion. I had dozens of friends, at least by my definition of the word *friend*. I couldn't imagine a life where I didn't have countless friends. Well, here I am. Not only can I now imagine that life, I am living it.

As a young child, everyone was my friend. I would count everyone in my class at school, everyone on my athletic teams, and everyone I knew from the neighborhood as my friend. A friend was really anyone that I knew who wasn't aggressively mean to me. As I aged, I became more discerning about who I would consider a close friend. However, I didn't conform to the trend of having a clique of friends. Many, if not most people, hang around people of a specific group. This is most common in high school. There are the jocks, the nerds, the thespians, the techies, etc. I, however, was "friends" with everyone. But in another sense, I was friends with no one. I collected friends like one might collect baseball cards. *The more the better* is what I thought. Unfortunately, this misperception left me feeling incomplete. Yes, people were friendly with me, but that doesn't mean that they were my friends. I had a misunderstanding about friendship that, if I'm honest with myself, has plagued me my entire life. Specifically, I thought that the more that I proved my worth, the more friends that I would have. I was intent on being the smartest, funniest, and most interesting person that I could be. I acted as though friends were a reward for high performance. In a sense, you could say that I was mistaking popularity with friendship.

Timothy 6:10 of the Bible states: "For the love of money is the root of all evil." Notice the phrase is not "money" is the root of all evil, but rather "the love of money." At the risk of sounding a bit melodramatic, I would contend a similar truth exists about popularity. I think it is fair to say that popularity is the currency of the youth. Just as there is nothing wrong with money, there is nothing wrong with being popular. However, although the love of popularity may not be the root of all evil, it is certainly not without some significant negative consequences. I warn you against falling into the trap of falling in love with popularity. I know of no one, myself included, who will tell you that this is a winning long-term strategy when it comes to developing and maintaining friendships. When you are in love with popularity you relish in "having" a lot of friends. Contrast this with the purer intention of "being" a good friend. There's a world of difference in this subtle distinction that I would encourage you to ponder.

Having friends is one thing, but being a friend is another. What does it mean to be a good friend? I had once heard that a friend is one who overlooks your broken fence and admires the flowers in your garden. I like this expression, but I would add that it is not enough to overlook your friend's broken fence—you must be vulnerable enough to expose your own broken fences to your friends. The tradeoff of getting to know someone well is that we become aware of their shortcomings, their warts, and their scars. The sacrifice that we make in return for having friends is increasing our vulnerability. Here is another problem I have encountered throughout my life. I know I have broken fences, but I am not comfortable talking about them. I am more inclined to hide my broken fences from even my closest friends. My reluctance to expose or even talk about my broken fences with friends has served as a barrier to developing long-lasting friendships. I am dancing around the topic of authenticity. Our closest friends extend the gift of vulnerability and share their most authentic selves.

A good friend shows up. Life milestones are a significantly important part of each of our lives. Graduation, marriage, kids' events, and death highlight the milestones in our lives. When our closest friends experience a life milestone, do your best to show up. It matters. Again, this is another shortfall of my own friendships, and I feel the divide that my absence has created. In my defense, I have moved all over the country since I was 20. This geographic distance combined with my military deployments resulted in me being an absentee friend for most of my life. Although my friends have extended me grace for my absence, there is no substitute for the presence of a friend.

A good friend lifts their friends up. There is a metaphor about friends' response to success that I have unfortunately witnessed. It's the "crabs in a bucket" metaphor. If you observe a bunch of crabs in a bucket, they exhibit a peculiar behavior when one of the crabs attempts to climb out of the bucket. Specifically, they pull the ambitious crab back into the bucket. Never pull your friend back into the bucket. This may sound obvious, but it is not. The harsh truth is that many people support their friends' success unless they perceive that success to be greater than their own. Imagine for a moment that you and your best friend both try out for the high school varsity baseball team. Your friend makes the team, but you don't. Can you genuinely celebrate your friend's success without a hint of envy? If you can, you are a great friend. If you can't, you are only human, but you have some work to do on your friendship skills. Related, a good friend lifts their friend's spirits and ambitions. *Yes, you can do it. Yes, you are talented. Yes, you are gifted.* Remember that each of us is cursed with an internal dialogue that haunts us with lies of criticism and self-doubt. A great friend remembers this and does their best to use their voice to cancel out the voices of their friend's demons.

Good friends know how to keep their mouths shut. Mark Twain said, "Two people can keep a secret if one of them is dead." Prove Mr. Twain wrong. Resist the temptation to gossip, especially about your friends. You will see other people do this often, but that doesn't make it right. A good friend knows that words exchanged between two people in private form an intimate bond that can last a lifetime. The quickest way to shatter this bond is to bring those words into the public eye. Be known as a friend that people can trust with a secret. As soon as you choose to break the confidence that was entrusted to you, know that your friend will find out; they always do.

A good friend knows how to forgive and forget. Human beings are imperfect. This includes even your closest friends. Inevitably, you will feel hurt and betrayed by a close friend. As Bob Marley once said, "The truth is, everyone is going to hurt you. You just got to find the ones worth suffering for." This is a matter of when, not if. Accept this now. That doesn't mean you should withhold your trust or vulnerability. What it does mean is that the benefits of having close friends outweigh the reality that you will be burned from time to time. When you are burned, you have an important choice to make. Will you forgive your friend or hold a grudge? There is probably no more noble gesture that you can make than to forgive your friend without conditions.

Close friends that you can grow old with are more than the spice of life, they are necessary ingredients. Good friends can feed your soul and color your life in ways for which there is no substitute. I'll leave you with the words of Henri Nouwen who wrote in *Out of Solitude: Three Meditations on the Christian Life*, "When we honestly ask ourselves which person in our lives means the most to us, we often find that it is those who, instead of giving advice, solutions, or cures, have chosen rather to share our pain and touch our wounds with a warm and tender hand. The friend who can be silent with us in a moment of despair or confusion, who can stay with us in an hour of grief and bereavement, who can tolerate not knowing, not curing, not healing and face with us the reality of our powerlessness, that is a friend who cares."

*Love,*
*Dad*

*Dear Hunter*

Over the course of my life, I have pondered the question: "What does it mean to be a man?" I recognize the sensitivity of this topic. Some may resist the validity of the question by rhetorically asking if the question of what it means to a man is different from the question of what it means to be human. I respect this viewpoint. However, just like there are modern day pressures placed on women, there are similar, but different, pressures placed on men. In the case of masculinity, what it means to be a "real man" is a question that, right or wrong, you will likely have to face. Although I have observed in my lifetime the rigid guideposts of masculinity to be dissolving, there remains some expectations that you will likely have to deal with. Let's deal, one at a time, with those expectations and stereotypes about what it takes to be a "real man."

Men should be physically strong. It does not take physical strength to be a real man. There is nothing wrong with being physically strong. Building your body through arduous exercise is great for your long-term physical and mental health as well as your self-esteem. However, a real man will never use his size or strength to intimidate others. A real man will never think less of someone because they are weaker than him. A real man will never make others feel like they are less than adequate because of their size and strength, or lack thereof. However, a real man is mentally strong. This strength manifests itself in a variety of contexts. An example includes having the strength to accept the consequences of his decisions. The universe is not stacked against you and it never will be. Most of our lives can be traced back to our decisions. A real man owns these decisions without excuse or complaint. Another example of mental strength is ability to withstand discomfort and uncertainty without panicking or complaining.

Men should be macho. That's horseshit, plain and simple. It is my experience and observation that macho men are the most insecure and insincere men around. As the poem *Desiderata* reminds us, "Avoid loud and aggressive persons; they are vexatious to the spirit." If, or rather when, you are forced to deal with a macho man, remember the saying, "Don't wrestle with a pig because you'll get dirty and the pig will like it." Don't stoop to their level, but don't back down. Develop a quiet confidence without a hint of machismo.

Men should hide their emotions. Pure baloney. A real man should be comfortable expressing the full range of human emotions. Yes, this includes crying. However, I do believe that a real man has control of his emotions; not a perfect amount of control, but a good amount of control. There is a difference between expressing your emotions in a healthy manner and being an emotional open book. There are some emotions that you should work to rein in, such as jealousy, envy, anger, hate, and greed. Even if you are feeling them, discipline yourself to minimize the outward appearance of these emotions. Additionally, consider how your display of emotions will impact others. For example, let's say that you receive a big promotion at work. However, two of your co-workers were up for the position as well. Demonstrating restraint in your emotional response is the prudent thing to do. You can jump for joy inside but demonstrate your respect for your co-workers by keeping a calm demeanor on the surface. A discipled approach to displaying your emotions is one of the most challenging skills to develop. There is nothing wrong with displaying a child-like wonder and curiosity about the world in which we live; however, when it comes to displaying your emotions, it is my belief that a real man has a more measured and mature approach. One of my favorite quotes regarding displaying emotion in response to achievement was from college football coach Joe Paterno who said, "Act like you expect to get into the end zone."

Men should be the dominant gender. As it pertains to your relationships with women, the word "dominant" should not be in your vocabulary. This is an antiquated notion that lingers only in the minds of the least evolved amongst us, but unfortunately, as I write this, it lingers nonetheless. As a real man, you will treat all women with the utmost respect. The same could be said of treating all people with the utmost respect. However, I think that we have to acknowledge that women do deal with disrespect from men disproportionately, and the actions of real men towards women have to account for this. What do I mean? Develop a reputation for being miles away from the "line" of inappropriate behavior and speech, especially in professional settings. In the workplace, avoid any type of flirtatious behavior whether you believe it is reciprocated or not. Sexual innuendos have no place in a professional setting. When in doubt, ask yourself if you would want someone to treat your sisters this way. Even if you have reason to believe that this type of behavior is not offensive to the person you are directing it towards, you are still wrong. For starters, you don't really know that this person is not uncomfortable with such behavior. Sadly, women have been putting up with inappropriate behavior from men their whole lives and some have learned to "grin and bear it." Additionally, this type of inappropriate behavior may make bystanders and observers uncomfortable. Lastly, it is my experience that nothing good ever comes from inappropriate behavior in the workplace. Eventually, the negative consequences will catch up with you. Of course, you don't avoid inappropriate behavior because of the consequences, you avoid it because it is the right thing to do.

Men don't ask for help. This statement could be made true with one additional word—*Stupid* men don't ask for help. Presumably, this sentiment originated from the idea that men should be independent. There is nothing wrong with seeking to be independent and refraining from playing the victim; in fact, I encourage you to do so. However, taking this to the extreme by refusing to ask for help when you need help is self-sabotaging behavior. I'm not talking about asking for directions when you're lost, (although I suppose in the age of GPS, this is an antiquated example). I am referring to instances in your life when you truly need help. For example, you may be suffering from a mental health episode or disorder and need help in addressing it. You may need help in addressing a developing addiction or other harmful behavior. Ask for help. The truth about help is that if you don't ask for it when you need it, you may very well get the help anyway when the situation degrades, but that help is rarely on your own terms. You are an imperfect, fallible human being, not a rock or an island. Think about when you are asked for help from someone else. Do you think less of that person? A real man musters the courage to ask for help when he needs it. A macho man is too cowardly to ask for help.

I grew up in an era when statements like these were still commonplace: *Real men don't cry. Suck it up. Act like a man. Grow a pair.* I don't imagine that you will be completely shielded from these mentalities, but I hope you will grow up with a balanced sense of what "act like a man" means. I have spent a good portion of my life pondering what this balanced sense looks like. I suppose I would have a different answer at each stage of my life. Perhaps this is not so much a progression of perspectives that are converging to the "right" answer but rather a reflection of the fact that life is composed of multiple chapters. In each of these chapters you, the main character, are a different person.

After much reflection on my own life, if asked today, "What is the manliest thing about you?" I would have an answer that I would probably surprise most people who know me. I wouldn't refer to my athletic or military achievements. I wouldn't reference a competitive spirit or toughness. Instead, I would say that the manliest thing about me is the acceptance of myself. I have come to peace, or am coming to peace, with who I am, which includes who I am not. That journey towards peace of mind comes with a realization of how challenging life can be for everyone. I am not in competition with my fellow man. I choose to view the world from a perspective of abundance, not scarcity; meaning the pie is big enough for us all to have a piece. It because of these perspectives that I can live with empathy, compassion, and kindness towards my fellow man. My journey to self-acceptance was not a well-paved path. It was mountainous and jagged. If there is anything about me that is rugged or tough, it is the mental spirit that has resulted from travelling this path.

*Love,*
*Dad*

*Dear Hunter*

The two words that have the greatest impact on your life are *yes* and *no*. These simple words will dictate the trajectory and quality of your life. When I reflect back on my life and my current circumstances, I find that my life is largely the sum of my use of the words *yes* and *no*.

About nine months before you were born, your mother and I were in Paris, France. We were sitting at an outdoor cafe at the world-famous art museum, the Louvre, enjoying coffee and pastries and looking out over the museum's courtyard. The conversation, like the Paris air, was breezy and comfortable. I don't remember how, but the conversation took a turn to a more serious topic—children. Your mother and I discussed bringing you into the world. After briefly considering the possibility, we said "yes" . . . to you. Less than a year later you were born, and our lives have been blessed in ways that we never could have imagined. All it took was saying, "yes" and rest, as they say, is history.

Early in my Navy career, I was an enlisted electronics technician and nuclear reactor operator. I was stationed in Orlando, Florida attending Navy Nuclear Power School. At this early stage in my Navy career, although I was enthralled with the challenges and missions that the Navy presented, I was also keen on earning a commission as a naval officer. This required me to be accepted into an officer program. My academic and military grades were the best in my class. The only thing that could keep me out of the officer program that I applied to was my own behavior—getting into some sort of trouble. After winning a championship softball game, the team was planning a celebratory night out. Unfortunately, some of the players were underage and that made me uncomfortable. The nuclear Navy was not known for giving out second chances when it came to underage drinking, and that included people who were of age and complicit in underage drinking. I remember like it was yesterday, pausing when asked, "DiGeronimo, you are joining us, right?" I took a beat to consider the question that was presented somewhat rhetorically. "No, I am going to pass." After a moderate amount of peer pressure aimed at getting me to change my mind, I returned to the barracks and spent the rest of the night reading a book in my rack. Long story short, the team found trouble. Every player in attendance was kicked out of the nuclear program and the handful of players in attendance at the celebration who had, like me, applied for an officer program were disqualified. I had dodged a bullet that would have changed the trajectory of my life, because of one word . . . *No*.

There are two distinct categories to the yes or no dilemma. One is life opportunities and experiences and the second is other people. It is my experience that most people, myself included, too frequently say "no" to life opportunities and "yes" to other people. There is, of course, overlap between these two categories, but they are distinct enough to discuss them separately.

The obstacle of saying "yes" to life opportunities is embedded in our DNA to some extent. The fear of the unknown and the uncertain typically stands in our way. This fear exists to protect us from the unknown threats hiding in the brush, waiting to attack us. This antiquated threat is perceived by our brains to be an existential threat. It is no small feat to overcome this hardwired fear, but you must if you are to live your best life in this modern world. They say opportunity knocks softly; I have found that it also often knocks only once. Unless you are prepared to say "yes" when you hear that opportunity knocking softly, the chances of saying "no" are high. Although we are predisposed to reject opportunities because we fear the unknown, all of life's greatest treasures are buried in the sands of the unknown. So how do we overcome our hardwired fear of the unknown and dig for our treasure chest?

The answer is twofold. First, you need to accept the fact that without deliberate effort and focus, you will naturally pass on life opportunities presented to you. Second, you need to practice saying "yes" to life. I recommend you start small. When the opportunity arises to try a new food, listen to a new band, or visit a new place, say "yes." Keep in mind that you won't reap the benefits of saying "yes" to new experiences if you are not fully invested. Keep your mind and heart open to these new experiences and embrace them fully. That is not to suggest that you will fall in love with the music of every new band that you listen to but give new experiences your full attention and your open mind.

The obstacle of saying "no" to other people is also evolutionary. Most of us are hardwired to be people-pleasers. This relates to our perceived value to our tribe. We innately desire an esteemed social standing, which is often derived from our ability or willingness to make other people happy. It should be no mystery why saying "no", especially to our friends and family, can be so difficult at times. However, you must learn to do exactly this. Your time is your most precious resource, and you should learn to treat it as such. Of course, you want to spend this resource on your friends and family, but you need to learn how to allocate your time so that you do not overcommit yourself. If you say "yes" to every request for your time, two things will invariably result. Number one, you will fail to meet your commitments. Number two, you will not have time to devote to yourself and your own dreams and goals.

Although this is true with friends and family, it is also exceedingly true when it comes to your professional relationships. Those who are successful in their academic careers and early in their professional life are especially prone to lack the will to say "no" to others. This stems from our early definition of success. In school, the syllabus is generally tried and true. Your professor is not going to intentionally give you more work than can possibly be completed. Therefore, we learn to tackle every task put on our academic plate with vigor. We are rewarded with good grades and positive feedback. The same is generally true early in our professional careers. However, a shift occurs as you progress in your career.

There will come a time when the work assigned to you grows beyond what you can reasonably tackle while maintaining the quality of work that you have grown accustomed to doing. This is an integral point in your career. If you haven't developed the ability and willingness to say "no," one or both of two things will occur. You will work yourself to a figurative death. You will put in crazy hours at the office or even bring your work home with you. Your weekends will evaporate. But even this will not be enough. Eventually, you will have to come to terms with the fact that there are only 168 hours in the week. Additionally, it is likely that the quality of your work will begin to suffer. If you are hell-bent on completing everything on your plate but are limited by the laws of time and space, you will have few options besides reducing the quality of your work. Often, this happens without you even realizing it.

Contrast this chain of events with someone in a similar professional position who knows when to say, "I can't tackle that assignment right now. I am already overloaded." The person who has learned to politely and professionally say "no," will not only protect their personal time; they will maintain the quality of their work. There is, of course, a fine line between communicating your limitations and coming across as incompetent. However, if you make no effort to find that line you will, in time, find yourself miles away from the line and drifting further each passing day.

I speak from experience regarding the professional consequences of not knowing how to say "no." My one entrepreneurial endeavor was moderately successful, but in retrospect the one thing that I would do differently would have been to say "no" more often. The Navy is not dissimilar from the academic world in that the workload. Although it can feel enormously heavy, it is well-defined and generally do-able. Therefore, when I launched my own company after retiring from the Navy, I had never really been forced to say "no" professionally before. My company was, at its core, a mergers & acquisitions company, but we expanded into other business services primarily because I couldn't say "no" to potential clients. *Do you offer this or that service? Sure, we do.* I fell into this trap because I confused what I could be doing with what I should be doing. They say that while there is no one recipe for success, there is certainly one for failure—and that is to try to please everyone.

Whether we are talking about your personal or professional life, or talking about life opportunities versus other people, the use of the words *yes* and *no* directly reflects your values, your priorities, and your vision. If these are not clearly formulated, you are likely to live like a Ping-Pong ball among a sea of other Ping-Pong balls. You will bounce from here to there due to external forces. Cultivate clearly formulated principles to counterbalance this tendency. You don't want to land where the winds take you; you want to land where you navigate yourself to.

*Love,*
*Dad*

*Dear Hunter*

American writer and artist Henry Miller said, "The only thing we never get enough of is love; and the only thing we never give enough of is love." Most of the quotes in this book are quotes that I have heard before. Admittedly, I had to search for this one because I didn't have any quotations about love committed to memory. For someone that considers themselves a walking quotation book, there was some irony in selecting this quote about love. How did I not have anything about love in my arsenal of quotations? Perhaps, in addition to never getting or giving enough love, there may be something to be said for the possibility that we don't think about love as much as we could or should.

We seek love and we give love, but what is love? Authors, poets, and artists have been trying to wrangle a definition of love for centuries. We seem to know when we feel it, but defining it is a bit of a challenge. I've thought a lot about this over the course of my life. The best that I have come up with is a metaphor that may be a bit strained, but it's the best that I have. Love is the cake of life where the ingredients are respect, grace, admiration, compassion, kindness, and empathy. Just like a cake is more than the sum of flour, butter, sugar, and eggs, love is more than the sum of its ingredients. And just like a cake wouldn't taste quite right if you removed one of the ingredients, love wouldn't feel quite right if you removed one of the ingredients. I like this metaphor, but it still feels incomplete. Is it possible to have all of the ingredients of love and somehow screw up the recipe? How can two people be in love one day and at each others' throats the next? How do people fall out of love? Can love last forever?

In second grade I was convinced that I was in love with a girl named Tracy. In sixth grade it was Jessica. In high school, my love belonged to my high school girlfriend, Jenni. In college, it was

Nicky. In the time between college and meeting your mother, there were others with whom I shared my love. In each instance, I was certain that I was "in love." In each instance, time has proved me to be incorrect. Or has it? Is love fleeting? Is love a transient emotion with evolutionary roots that has us confused? When the "magic" fades, what is actually fading? I ask more questions than I answer because this reflects my knowledge on the subject — more questions than answers. However, I have a few lessons that I think I can pass along to you. One is that true love is a much more sophisticated and nuanced emotion than we typically assume. At each stage of my life, what it meant to be in love was different than the previous stage. Clearly, the love of my 2nd grade crush was not an equivalent love to that which I share with your mother. I think we learn more and more about love as we age. Here are some of the lessons that I have learned:

- Love is an action verb, first and foremost. Love, as a feeling upon which to be inebriated, is fleeting. It is wonderful, splendid, and one of life's strongest emotions, but I have come to believe that this intoxicating feeling can only take a relationship so far. When people expect that feeling to survive the years, they are invariably disappointed. That type of love is like a puppy. It's brand new, it's cute, it's playful, and we can't get enough of it. Puppies age. Love matures. As love matures, it requires more attention and nurturing to survive. If we consider love an action verb versus a feeling, we attend to the object of our love in a manner that is more consistent with the notion of love being a selfless act. If I "know" anything about love it is this — true love is when we commit ourselves to the action of loving without expectations or conditions. Several times in this book, I have discussed the misconception about the relationship between action and motivation. Specifically, the flawed idea that motivation drives action. The truth is that action spawns motivation. Similarly, the emotion of love follows the act of love, not the other way around. Related, remember that actions speak louder than words. As Ralph Waldo Emerson said, "What you do speaks so loudly that I cannot hear what you say.." At the end of your life, your love will be measured and remembered by your actions, not your words.

- Lao Tzu said, "Being deeply loved by someone gives you strength, while loving someone deeply gives you courage." This is a beautiful sentiment. However, I would contend that loving someone deeply requires courage as much as it may give you courage in return. If you choose to live your life with love as I hope you do, your heart is going to be broken. The first cut will be the deepest. Many people never fully recover from this first cut. They build walls around themselves with bricks of cynicism and distrust. This is the easy way out and is a surefire recipe to sabotage future relationships. You can choose to protect yourself or you can choose love, but you can't have both. Choosing to love freely and fully even after you have been hurt is the courageous response for which life rewards those brave enough to seek it.

- Self-love is the prerequisite to all other forms of love. How do you know when you are ready to experience the fullness of love and all that it has to offer? I don't know. But what I do know is that if you don't love yourself, you are not ready to love someone else. It is a losing and unfair strategy to have your self-worth dependent upon the love of someone else. It is my experience that this creates a fragile love that rarely, if ever, lasts. So instead of wondering when you will meet the love of your life, wonder instead how you can prepare yourself for the love of your life. This preparation is 90 percent self-love.  You must truly love yourself before you can reap the wonders of another's love. I recognize that this could be perceived as a narcissistic sentiment; however, that is not my intent. Consider the ingredients of love that I referenced earlier in this letter:  respect, grace, admiration, compassion, kindness, and empathy.  Become an expert at extending these emotions to yourself before you can expect someone else to do the same.  I have been guilty of using other people's love as a substitution for the love that I didn't feel for myself, and I can tell you categorically that pursuing this strategy is a dead end.

- Not all true love is romantic love.  I've focused this letter on the love of romance.  However, keep your heart open to love for all those closest to you.  Your family loves you unconditionally in a way that is beautiful but also hard to comprehend.  Family love creates one of, if not the, strongest bonds of love. I think of my brother and sister, who I am ten and thirteen years older than, respectively.  When I left the house at the age of 18, they were still little kids.  My life decisions weren't conducive to being around the house that much after I left for college.  Life in the Navy had me thousands of miles away for birthdays, graduations, sporting events, and holidays. Yet, somehow, love persisted.  I have a very special bond with my brother and sister to this day.  I know that you will share a special love with your sisters.  Treat this love with respect, for it is one of the most treasured forms of love on Earth.  Unfortunately, I have known people who have had a falling-out with their siblings.  Sometimes, this results in siblings not talking for extended periods of time.  No matter what the argument was about, I've never known anyone who was in this position who didn't regret allowing an argument to damage the family bond of love.

Hunter, I would be remiss in a letter about love to not remind you that I love you with all of my heart. My love for your mother, your sisters, and you is not conditional, temporary, or partial. I share this love with you and our family with every ounce of me. I will always love you with my entire being and my entire heart, no matter what. There is nothing that you have to do to earn my love. There is nothing you could do to lose my love.

*Love,*
*Dad*

P.S. - I intentionally did not mention love from your parents. This is a whole separate category of love to which I have devoted the next letter. Truth to be told, this love is so powerful there should be a separate word for it.

*Dear Hunter*

This letter is one of the most difficult letters in this book for me to write. Primarily, because the emotions that I have felt since becoming your parent and the emotions that I feel towards my own parents are so deep and complex that they are almost indescribable. I feel like I have so much to tell you regarding the parent and child relationship. However, when I sit down to write about it, the words escape my grasp like a wisp of smoke from an extinguished candle.

If I were to re-write this letter a year from now, five years from now, or twenty years from now, it would be a different letter. I acknowledge that parenting is a journey of self-discovery and I am in the journey's beginning stages. I've been on my fair share of life journeys but I have never been as excited about one as I am about the journey of being your father. In the short time that I have had the privilege to call myself your father, I have learned volumes about myself and about life. People have always told me that when you have kids your perspective on life changes. I figured that was just something that parents said. I didn't really expect my whole outlook on life to change. After all, I had seen children before. In fact, being many years older than my brother and sister, I watched them grow up. I thought, *I get it.* Wow, was I wrong. The first shift in my perspective related to my perception of and relationship with my own parents.

The American minister Henry Ward Beecher said, "We never know the love of a parent till we become parents ourselves." It's funny how the love that I feel for my parents has increased tenfold since you were born. I never realized just how deep a love could be before you came into the world. Experiencing these emotions over the past few years has given me a humbling amount of appreciation, respect, and admiration for my own parents. We tend to see our parents through a lens of perfection. Our parents are supposed to know everything, including how to be a parent. But why on God's green Earth would this be true? I remember bringing you home from the hospital and thinking, "What the hell is going on? They just let us leave with a brand new human being?! No instructions, no test, no safety net. *Here is a human being for you to take care of. Good luck!* I can tell you that I have never been more terrified in my life. I immediately thought about my own parents.

When you were born, I was 44 years old. I had spent 20 years in the Navy conducting clandestine nuclear submarine missions vital to national security. During this time, I travelled the world and the seven seas. You might think I was prepared to handle parenthood. I wasn't. My parents were 21 when I was born. 21!? When I left the house at age 18, my parents were 39. They raised me to adulthood at an age younger than I was when you were born! Any complaints or dissatisfaction that I had about their parenting vanished when I began to experience parenthood for myself. They did their best at the world's most challenging assignment. Truth be told, their best was incredible. To this day, I wonder where they learned to be parents. They always seemed to know the right answer and how to handle complex or messy situations. Behind the scenes, they were probably just as insecure about parenting as I am, but they hid it well. Parents are not born as parents.

Another life-altering perspective that your birth made clear to me is that you will never be "ready" to be a parent. This is true for many life events. It is never the perfect time to get married, to buy a house, to move, or to switch jobs. Parenthood is no exception. When I was in my twenties, the idea of being a parent was foreign to me. I had peers in the Navy who had children but I couldn't wrap my brain around how they could be parents at such a young age. As I found, it doesn't matter what age you have children. You will never feel ready.

However, don't sell yourself short, either. As I mentioned before, parenthood is terrifying, but I am finding out that in some ways I have been preparing myself to be a father for my entire adult life. As you live your life, your values, priorities, and beliefs are formulated. These are the guiding principles that you will use as a parent. Solidifying who you are as a person and what you believe in is all the preparation that you need for parenthood.

There are only two things that I can give you as a father. One is me. The real me. The best of me. The other is my time. My father often talked about the importance of being physically present for family. I recall him saying that professional sacrifices were worth their cost if it meant he was home for dinner each night. I kind of understood what he meant pre-parenthood, but now I fully understand. When you were born, I was the Vice President of Operations for an energy company. My position required me to oversee the operation of power plants throughout the United States. I was living out of a suitcase. Without exception, I was getting on a plane early Monday morning and then returning on Thursday evening. This was my job. However, it became clear to me that being home for dinner and to help tuck you into bed each night was more important to me than any professional opportunity. Long story short, to make that happen, I switched career paths entirely. My new position as the General Manager of a facility that makes and prints corrugated boxes isn't the sexiest position I've had in my lifetime, but it affords me the opportunity to come home to you, your sisters, and your mother each night. At the end of the day, the most precious and impactful thing that we have to share with our children is our time.

I have never felt more vulnerable in all of my life than I do now as a parent. I have lived a life of "rugged individualism" where I was never too worried about landing on my feet. I am generally not a worrier. I have always had faith in my own abilities to handle whatever life may throw at me. However, now that I am a parent, I find myself feeling more vulnerable than I ever could have imagined. The thought of losing my job makes my heart skip a beat. I am more concerned about the economy and world politics than I have been before. Climate change, inflation, crime rates, viruses, war, famine - all of these threats have existed in the world for my entire life, yet it wasn't until I became a parent that they affected my ability to sleep well at night. Although these feelings aren't pleasant, being a father has made me feel more connected to the world than I ever have before. I think about the world that you will inherit. I think about the planet that you will inhabit. As I think about these things, I realize that in some metaphysical sense, you are my connection to humanity's future. I do not expect to "know" if there is an afterlife before my last breath, but watching you grow and develop has given me a sense of immortality. I sense how my DNA and my experiences live on. I sense how my presence may continue to be felt by the world after I pass. Pretty cool, huh? Laugh now if you read this before you have children, but get back to me if you are still laughing after you do.

As strange, or perhaps as obvious as it may sound to you, your mother and I are very ordinary human beings with no special parenting skills or training. We were babies, toddlers, and children once ourselves. We have fears, imperfections, and insecurities. All we have to give you is our best. There is not much about life that I can promise you, but please know that your mother and I will always give you our best. There will be times, I suppose, when our best may not seem good enough. There will be times when we get something wrong. There will be times when you get frustrated or angry with us. I know this, because I felt it as a child myself. But I am telling you from the bottom of my heart and soul, your mother and I have never committed ourselves more fully to any endeavor in our lifetimes than that of being parents to you and your sisters. I could tell you this every day for the rest of our life, but I suppose that until you have children of your own, you won't fully appreciate the depth of this promise.

*Love,*
*Dad*

*Dear Hunter*

September 11, 2001. I was 27 years old and serving aboard the fast attack nuclear submarine, USS Hampton (SSN-767) in Norfolk, Virginia. We were scheduled to get underway for a few weeks to conduct training exercises in preparation for our next deployment. I was the officer in charge of conducting the reactor startup that morning. The reactor startup commenced at 5 o'clock in the morning and had proceeded as expected without any hiccups. Towards the end of the startup procedure, one of my peers came into the engine room's control room.

"I am here to relieve you. You need to go see the Chief Engineer," he said.

I chuckled.

"What?! In the middle of a reactor startup?"

I was certain he was kidding. He wasn't. I checked the clock on the control room wall. It was 9:13 a.m. I made an entry in the reactor logbook documenting my departure and left to see the Engineer.

As I walked from the engine room to the Engineer's stateroom, I passed the area of the submarine called the crew's mess. This is where the crew ate their meals. I was expecting to see the normal hustle and bustle of breakfast time. Instead, I sensed the energy of the crew to be unusual. Excuse the Star Wars reference, but I felt a disturbance in the force. The crew was captivated by something that was airing on the news. I paused briefly to join them. Something about an airplane that had crashed into the World Trade Center. I was remarkably unphased and continued on my way. *Probably a small Cessna plane that lost its way.*

As I walked into the Engineer's stateroom, the pieces of the puzzle were slowly coming together in my obstinate mind. The look on this salty senior officer's face remains seared into my memory to this day — as serious as I have ever seen him look.

"Call home and make sure that your family is okay," he said.

"Huh?" I replied.

"I don't know the details, but it appears that New York City is under attack. We are still getting underway and phone lines will be cut in a few minutes," he stated as he left the room.

I understood the words that he was saying to me, but I couldn't process them. I glanced at the phone affixed to the stateroom wall. My hand grabbed the receiver and my fingers dialed a phone number, but my mind was still stuck on the consequences of the words, "New York City is under attack." My parents lived in New Jersey just a few miles outside of New York City, so my mind was conjuring some disturbing images that quickly subsided when my mother answered the phone.

"Hello?"

"Hi, Mom. It's Matt. Is everything okay? What is going on? We are getting underway soon and I can't talk for long."

Calmly and collectively, my mother assured me that everyone was accounted for but couldn't fill in the details yet about what was happening in New York City. "The towers have collapsed, but we are all okay."

As I hung up the phone, I took a deep breath and closed my eyes. I still didn't know what was happening or why, but I was sure of one thing, my life had just changed forever. 9/11 of 2001 would forever be remembered as the day that terrorists hijacked planes and flew them into the World Trade Center in New York City and the Pentagon in Washington, D.C. More than 3,000 people were killed on this infamous day in American history.

In the aftermath of 9/11, my life did change forever. Since the bombing of Pearl Harbor in 1941, the United States had protected its citizens and land from an enemy attack. The streak had ended and, with it, the peace of mind that American citizens had enjoyed in my lifetime.

In early 2003, my tour of duty aboard the USS Hampton had come to an end. It was time for me to go on shore duty. Shore duty is an assignment that breaks up sea tours because life on a submarine is only tolerable for a few years at a time. Typically, shore duty is an assignment as an instructor, an inspector, or a staff officer. With a current war in Afghanistan and another war on the horizon with Iraq, I felt compelled to volunteer for an assignment in the Middle East. I wanted to support the war efforts in any way that I could. The Navy granted me my wish. I was assigned to the staff of Commander Middle East Force based out of the small island nation of Bahrain.

I readily volunteered for this assignment and enthusiastically moved to the other side of the planet for 18 months because we were the good guys. We were good guys fighting evil. The bad guys had to pay for what they did on 9/11. The differentiation between good and bad was black and white to me in those days. As the years passed, my hair grayed and so did my perspective.

In war it is challenging, if not impossible, to draw clear lines of right or wrong, black or white, good or evil. Knowing what I know now about the politics of the wars in the Middle East, do I still believe that we were the good guys fighting the bad guys? Hmm. Yes . . . ish.

It is estimated that 206,000 civilians were killed in Iraq from 2003 through 2021. 206,000! That carnage is the equivalent of 68 9/11 attacks. If you were a civilian living in Iraq and your family was killed by United States forces as a casualty of war, who would you call the "bad" guys? I don't present these figures to make the case that the United States represented the bad guys, but when we talk about good versus evil, often the lines that we draw are a matter of perspective.

Does evil exist in the world? I don't know—truly. I certainly know that evil, heinous acts and behavior exist, but I don't know if I believe that people are evil. Perhaps the distinction is irrelevant. A valid question remains. what is good, and how is it different from evil? My opinion that I will share with you is that good is the existence of empathy, and true evil is the lack of empathy. I believe that we are all born with the propensity to feel empathy. However, some of us lose the courage to act upon it. For example, would it be enough to say that a Nazi working at a concentration camp wasn't evil because he felt empathy for the Jewish people that were captured, worked to near death, and then exterminated? Clearly not. The Nazi behavior is among the evilest in recorded history and it reflects, in my opinion, the lack of courage exhibited by the Nazi army to act on the empathy for the Jewish people that was transcribed on their souls at birth.

This discussion becomes very complex and philosophical very quickly when you start to ask yourself if the "ends justify the means." For example, would you kill one innocent family if it meant that you would save the lives of thousands? There are books devoted to this subject which I will not try to tackle in this letter, but you can see that defining good versus evil is not always as simple as it is made out to be. However, I would warn you against using the "ends justify the means" in your daily life. I have observed this to be the ultimate character trap—rationalization that can convince you that behavior that is not consistent with your values is justifiable.

Another angle to view the battle of good versus evil which is perhaps more likely to impact you directly in your life is expressed by Edmund Burke. He said, "The only thing necessary for the triumph of evil is for good men to do nothing." You see, my son, good people will always outnumber bad people in this beautiful and miraculous world of ours. However, good does not always triumph over evil because sometimes the good people choose not to get involved. It is not enough to consider yourself a good person unless you can translate your empathy for others into action. This is true even when the action required is uncomfortable, inconvenient, or at times dangerous. Of course, you can't spend your life rescuing every stray dog that you come across. However, learn to trust your intuition when life presents you with defining moments. Defining moments are those that the universe places in your path to allow you to take a character temperature check. As Kevin Costner's character Roy McAvoy said in the movie Tin Cup, "When a defining moment comes along, you define the moment... or the moment defines you."

*Love,*
*Dad*

*Dear Hunter*

When I was a student in high school, I wanted to graduate as the class valedictorian. I wanted this so badly that I sacrificed time with friends and family. I wanted this so badly that I wasn't always my authentic self with my peers and teachers. I was obsessed with my grades. If someone tried to talk to me about maintaining better "balance" in my life, I would have scoffed at the notion. Anything worth fighting for was going to upset the balance in my life.

This trend of pursuing goals with every ounce of my energy continued for a substantial amount of my adult life. I had an "all-or-nothing" mentality. When I was studying Nuclear Engineering at Rensselaer Polytechnic Institute (RPI), I wanted to graduate with a 4.0 grade point average. When I was attending the Navy's Nuclear Power School, I wanted to graduate as the class "Honor Man." I poured my heart and soul into these efforts to achieve what I believed to be the ultimate goal in life . . . being the best at whatever I did. In hindsight, I believe that I was getting part of the equation right, but falling flat on another part. Specifically, there is nothing wrong with striving for grand achievements and goals. It is admirable, noble, and valiant to strive to be the best in whatever you do. However, I have learned that this effort is only sustainable when accomplished through a balanced approach and mentality. Further, it is a losing strategy to base your standing as the "best" exclusively through external validation sources such as grades and achievements. The man in the mirror is your competition as well as your source of validation, no one else.

In 2006, I was assigned to serve as the Chief Engineer aboard the fast-attack nuclear submarine, the USS Key West (SSN-722). The engineering department of that submarine had a reputation for being in need of drastic operational improvement. During the submarine's previous annual inspection called an ORSE (Operational Reactor Safeguards Examination) the submarine was deemed to be "safe" to continue to operate nuclear power. However, when compared to other submarines in the fleet, their grade was the lowest possible grade. I took it upon myself to reinvigorate the department and propel them as the "best" engineering department in the fleet. I was "all in" in my efforts to do so. The department responded positively to my leadership efforts. In-port, we had completed many complex maintenance procedures gracefully, professionally, and on-time. At-sea, our ability to operate the nuclear power plant through a series of complex evolutions, drills, and operations improved dramatically. Additionally, our training program had become one of the most robust programs that I had ever been a part of and the academic grades of the department reflected this improvement. As importantly, at least in hindsight, was the fact that the morale of the department had improved drastically. The department no longer felt like the chew-toy of the fleet. I could see the confidence and pride in the members of the department shining through on a daily basis.

A year had passed and we were about a month away from our next inspection. I was laser-focused on getting the highest possible grade on the inspection. It had become my Moby Dick. We were conducting practice drills on the reactor plant. I had stepped out of the control room for a moment and when I came back into the room, the reactor operator was furiously erasing something that he had written on the reactor plant panel in grease pencil. When I asked what he had written, he was reluctant to tell me. After some prodding, he confessed that he had written the "average." Why? Because, as he explained it, that was his hope for our grade on this upcoming inspection. He felt that if we got a higher grade, the pressure would be too high for us to maintain our standard. If we got a lower grade, the pressure would remain high for us to increase our standard. In hindsight, he wasn't wrong. At a minimum, reasonable people could disagree on this point. However, I was not in a reasonable mindset. I had him immediately relieved from his duties as reactor operator. I laid into him verbally as I have seldom, if ever, done before or since. In fact, I had him wash dishes in the galley for the next two weeks. *No one who strives to be "average" is going to be a member of this team,* I thought to myself.

The inspection came and went and we received a very high grade. The waterfront staff was remarkably impressed and I felt like I had landed my Moby Dick. However, what I failed to realize at the time was that we had accomplished what we had aimed to accomplish before the inspection team even stepped foot aboard the submarine. We turned the department around in a remarkable way. Everyone, including the reactor operator that I had washing dishes, had done their part in accomplishing this. The inspection grade reflected our efforts, but I should never have let the inspection validate our worth, or more specifically, my worth. I lost my balance and proportion in my leadership skills because I was enamored with the fools' gold of external validation from an inspection team.

Years later, the glow of the inspection grade has faded. What remains is the feeling I have regarding my true assignment aboard that submarine, which was to lead and inspire members of the engineering department. Although I remain proud of what we accomplished, it is clear to me that I could have been a better leader, mentor, and role model if I wasn't so laser-focused on an inspection grade. I lost sight of the fact that the people in the department had families, friends, and lives outside of the submarine. I lost sight of the fact that my ability to impact the lives of the engineering department would extend beyond our time on that submarine. I lost sight of maintaining balance in the approach to my assignment.

The Navy didn't help me develop the balance in my life that I have since found. I am not blaming the Navy for this, but the structure of the Navy enabled me to continue to manically strive for the gold medal. Assignments in the Navy only last a few years. I have found that I can sprint at a frantic pace for a few years at a time, but I have also discovered that eventually there is a price to pay for living a life without balance. I have to believe that this price is different for each of us. For me, the price was in the form of my mental and physical health, and my peace of mind. Eventually, I hit a wall while running at a hundred miles an hour. Anyone who knew me could have probably predicted it.

I was forced to realize that I had spent most of my life on a figurative treadmill chasing a treasure on the other side of the room. I was ensconced in a blanket of blacks and whites. I knew "all" and I knew "nothing". Anything in between was a place for losers, as far as I was concerned. To live a life of balance was to live a life of mediocrity. I was a battleship beached on dry land. I had been scratching and clawing to fight an enemy that wasn't there. In doing so, I was turning my back on modern day society's great luxury — the ability to live a harmonious life. We are not living in a war-torn nation. We are not suffering through a famine. I know now that a life of balance is a prerequisite to a harmonious life.

In her book, *Eat, Pray, Love*, Elizabeth Gilbert writes, "The ingredients of both darkness and light are equally present in all of us,...The madness of this planet is largely a result of the human being's difficulty in coming to virtuous balance with himself. " For me, the roadblock to achieving this balance has always been the need for achievement. I was willing to do whatever I had to do to scratch this itch. The problem was not my desire for achievement. The problem was not my willingness to do whatever needed to be done. You can, and should, be driven and ambitious while also living a balanced and harmonious life. The key for me has been to fall in love with the journey, not the destination. When you realize that the road down which you are travelling is not a means to an end, it in and of itself is the end, I have observed a natural tendency to embrace a balanced approach to life. Resist the temptation to race towards the pot of gold at the end of the rainbow. Instead ,slow your pace and enjoy the view of the rainbow.

*Love,*

*Dad*

*Dear Hunter*

My series of letters and this book are drawing to an end. I have enjoyed every moment of writing this book and I hope that you have enjoyed reading it. As I reflect on the letters that I have written, there is one area of life that I have been remiss in not emphasizing. That area is family. Specifically, your family. If you were to strip down life to its essentials, I think you would find that the list is pretty short — food, shelter, and family; not necessarily in that order. We are beyond blessed to have the family that we do. You have an incredible group of people to call your family. You have an incredible group of people that love you very much. The most wonderful part of family is that you don't earn their love, you revel in it, and you return it just as you received it — unconditionally. Further, you have something valuable to learn from every person in your family that I would like to share with you. It would require at least another full book to describe your family and their virtues, so I will attempt to only hit the highlights for you in this letter.

Your mother, Caroline. Where to start? She stole my heart with her smile the day that I met her in a small breakfast cafe in Oak Park, Illinois. Her beauty and grace are matched only by her inner beauty. She has the kindest heart you will ever meet. Her devotion to her family knows no bounds. She is a devoted friend, sister, and daughter. Her ears and heart are always open to a friend or family member in need. She has an unmatched generosity of spirit. She is my partner in parenting and in life and I thank God every day for this. I know you inherited your smile from your mother and I am hopeful that you inherit her kindness, compassion, and capacity for love.

Your oldest sister, Addison. Addison is 13 years older than you. She is intelligent, thoughtful, and brave. She is the most talented writer in the family and a devoted and graceful dancer. Addison has extremely high emotional intelligence. I tell her that the song, "Vienna" by Billy Joel is her song, as it is clear to me that Vienna truly does wait for her. From Addison, I hope you inherit emotional intelligence and writing ability.

Your youngest sister, McKenna. McKenna is 10 years older than you. She is fun-loving, adventurous, and kind. I have watched McKenna embrace many different endeavors such as crafting, painting, baking, soccer, basketball, volleyball and tennis. She is always up for a good joke or prank. From McKenna, I hope you inherit a sense of humor and adventurous spirit.

Your grandma, Theresa. I could, and should, write a book about your grandma. She has already lived an incredible life and shows no signs of slowing down. I could not have asked to be blessed with a better mother. She has given so much of herself to her family without ever breathing a word about her sacrifices. Somehow, in addition, she is a prolific and award-winning author, teacher, professor, and librarian. No one knows how she does it, but she does. Sometimes it feels like she is working with more hours in the day than the rest of us, and the exclamation point of it all is that she makes it look so easy. I am truly in awe of her and humbled to call her my mother. She is my hero. I hope that you inherit her loving spirit, her selfless devotion to family, and her ability to make grand achievements look effortless.

Your grandpa, Mick. There is no man that has impacted my development into the man that I am today more than your grandpa. His heart is as big as God makes hearts. His work ethic is without peer and has been the yardstick with which I measure my own efforts throughout my life. He is one of, if not the, best athletes I have ever known in my life; his God-given athletic ability is off the charts. He is also blessed with a sharp and curious intellect that has challenged me my entire life. Your grandpa is also one of the most likeable people around. Everyone loves your grandpa! He is also my hero. I hope that you inherit his curious nature, his giving spirit, and charismatic personality.

Your Bebe, Beth. Your Bebe is an old soul with a nurturing spirit and the patience of a saint. She is beloved by her family as well as the hundreds of students she has taught as a career elementary school teacher. She is ultra-organized, considerate, and compassionate. I have never met a less judgmental person in all of my life. She accepts people as they are and looks for the good in others and in life. I hope that you inherit her patience, her compassion, and her nurturing nature.

Your Papa, John. Your Papa is larger than life! He is the life of the party and the energy in every room in which he enters. He values family above all else and is a very principled and dedicated man. When he commits to something, there is no halfway. He is "all in" in every endeavor. As a devoted fan of baseball and football, his Indians and Browns often break his heart, but he's as loyal as the day is long. I hope that you inherit his energy, his loyalty, and his love of family.

Your Uncle Joey. Joey inherited your grandpa's athletic abilities. Outside of the family, he has a reputation as one of the best athletes to ever come out of Hawthorne, New Jersey. Inside of the family, we know him as pensive, empathetic, and courageous. He has devoted his life to the safety and security of the public as a police officer and detective. A devoted father to your cousin Anthony, Joey knows how to make children of all ages smile. Along with his insightful nature, his emotional intelligence is off the charts. You can always rely on Uncle Joey to make you laugh and to make you think. I hope that you inherit his courage, his thoughtfulness, and his power of observation.

Your Aunt Colleen.  Your Aunt Colleen is a tough nut to crack.  She often appears quiet and reserved, but we all know that she is painfully funny and extremely outgoing when she chooses to be. She is the one in the family with the musical and artistic talent.  As a child and young adult, she dazzled us on the piano.  As an adult, her ability to artistically represent complex ideas through art, words, and color has made her a world-class graphic designer. She has a flare for embracing all that life has to offer in a balanced and harmonious manner.  Your Aunt Colleen is a rock of dependability and rock star of anything that she touches.   I hope that you inherit her sense of humor, her reliability, and her tender heart.

Your Uncle Brett. Your Uncle Brett loves cars, sports, and his family. He, like his father, possesses an incredible work ethic and devotion to his family.  He, like his mother, is an old soul with patience, kindness, and compassion for others.  Your Uncle Brett is an avid sports fan and loyal to the Browns, Indians, and Ohio State University football. He was a great athlete himself. He is a dedicated father to your cousins Brady, Connie, and Ben.   I hope that you inherit his sense of family values, professional dedication, and fun loving spirit.

Your Aunt Brittany.  Your Aunt Brittany is full of life and a ball of energy.  She is the most engaging member of your family, as she has a way of making anyone with whom she is talking feel like the most important person on Earth.  It is this characteristic combined with genuine compassion and empathy that makes her such a skilled and valued nurse.  She is an incredible and devoted mother to your cousins Gibson and Scarlett.  I hope that you inherit her sense of empathy, engaging soul, and zest for life.

This is your immediate family, your tribe.  They all love you so very much and we are blessed to call them our "home team."  If you notice, there is a commonality in my descriptions. Specifically, the devotion to family. Friends will make appearances in your life, but most will fade away. Family is forever. In the words of the French author, Andre Maurois, "Without a family, man, alone in the world, trembles with the cold." You, my son, are blessed with the shelter of a strong family and will never tremble in the cold.

*Love,*
*Dad*

# $\mathcal{A}$bout the $\mathcal{A}$uthor

Photo by Mónica F. García

Matthew DiGeronimo is a native of Hawthorne, NJ. His life experiences include submarine officer for the United States Navy, entrepreneur, radio talk show host, college adjunct professor, energy and manufacturing operations executive, artist, and author. He holds an undergraduate degree in nuclear engineering from Rensselaer Polytechnic Institute (RPI) and an MBA from the University of Connecticut. He resides in Oak Park, Illinois with his wife Caroline, his step-daughters Addison and McKenna, his son Hunter, and his two dogs, Ruby and Teddy.

To contact Matt, visit MattDiGeronimo.com or email him at matt.digeronimo@gmail.com

Made in the USA
Middletown, DE
08 July 2021